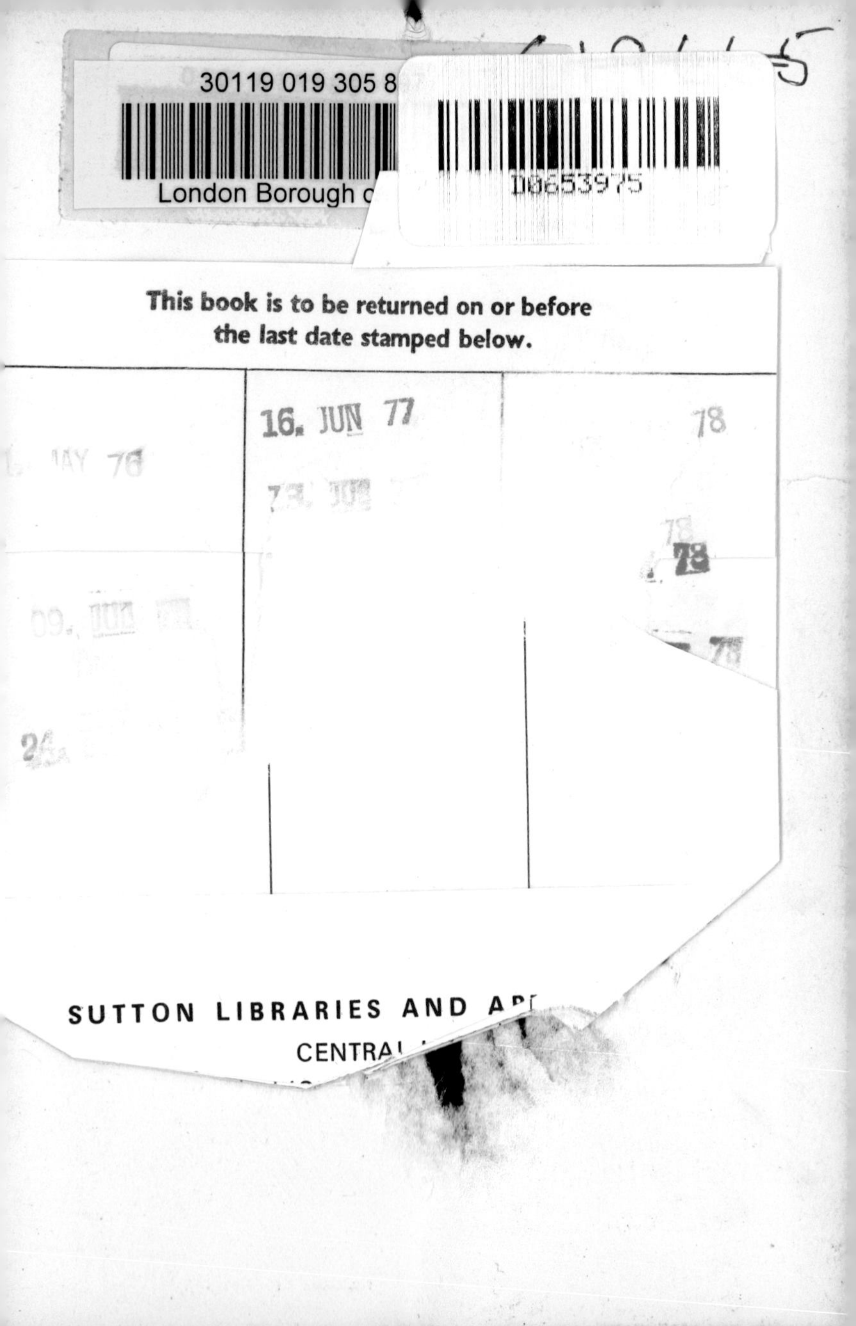

Exploring Education

The

Gifted Child

The Gifted Child

by

J. B. Shields
B.A., M.Ed.

Principal Lecturer in Education,
St. John's College, York.

National Foundation for Educational Research
in England and Wales
The Mere, Upton Park, Slough, Bucks.

Published by the National Foundation for Educational Research in England and Wales

The Mere, Upton Park, Slough, Bucks and at 79 Wimpole Street, London, W.1

First Published 1968

Second Impression 1968

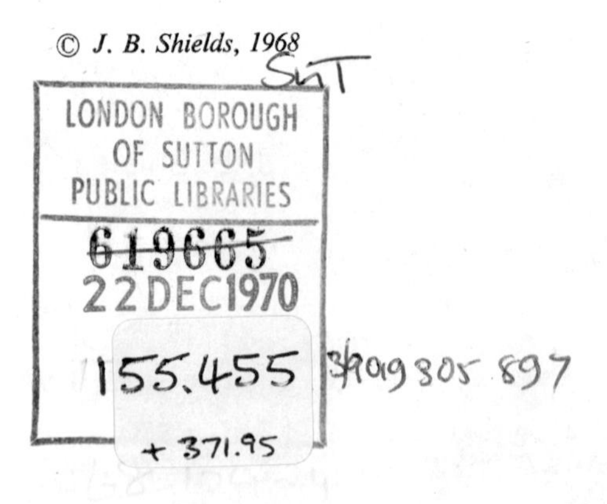

Cover Design by Bryan Austin

Printed in Great Britain by
KING, THORNE & STACE LTD., SCHOOL ROAD, HOVE BN3 5JE

Contents

Preface

I have had two aims in writing this book. First, to bring together in a convenient form some of the findings of research studies of the gifted child. Second, to present the findings in such a way as to bring out their significance for teachers, students and parents, and indeed any person concerned about the education of children.

I wish to thank Dr. K. Lovell, of the University of Leeds, for his kindness in reading the manuscript, and for the corrections and additions which he suggested. At the same time I must make it clear that the text is my own responsibility.

The publication of this book allows me the opportunity to express my thanks to many people who made possible my own research studies; Dr. Lovell, the children who were the subjects of the investigation, the chief education officers, and the heads and teachers in the schools. I wish also to thank many colleagues and friends for their interest and help.

April, 1968 J. B. SHIELDS

Chapter One

The Problem of Definition

THE term 'gifted child' is frequently used to signify a child who has obtained an outstandingly high score on a standardized test of intelligence. A child with a high IQ is a gifted child.

This particular use of the term is associated with the work of Professor L. M. Terman of Stanford University, California, who applied it, over forty years ago, to a group of children he was studying and wrote about in *The Mental and Physical Traits of a Thousand Gifted Children*. In the early years of the century, Terman, who had obtained a doctorate degree from Clark University for a study of the intellectual abilities of seven bright and seven dull boys, formed the idea of studying a large group of highly intelligent children. He wished the group to be large enough for firm conclusions to be drawn. One of his problems was to find a means of choosing a large number of children who would be 'reasonably representative of intellectually gifted children' (op. cit. 1926). This was indeed a formidable task. Terman had, however, in the preceding years been very impressed with the scale of tests of intelligence devised by the Parisian psychologists Binet and Simon. Constructed to deal with the problem of identifying children of very low mental ability, it impressed Terman by its worth in identifying children of very high mental ability: 'The value of the Binet method in the identification of the intellectually gifted became immediately evident to the writer when with Mr. H. G. Childs he made trial of the 1908 scale' (op. cit

1926). So Terman set to work to produce a scale of his own based upon the Binet method. A new concept used in the Binet Scale was that of 'mental age'. From a pupil's performance upon the test it was possible to say if his mental abilities were equal to, better than, or not so good as those of the average pupil of the same age. If a child aged ten years achieved a performance equal to that of the average child of the same age he was declared to have a mental age of ten years; likewise if his performance equalled that of the average pupil two years older he was ascribed a mental age of twelve years, and other mental ages were calculated in the same way. It may be noted that the relationship of mental age to chronological age in terms of advance or retardation gave a convenient frame of reference for children's abilities. Terman used this method of compiling mental ages, but he also adopted the use of the 'intelligence quotient'. This technique allowed him to show the ratio of mental age to chronological age in terms of a score which was calculated in the following manner:

$$\frac{\text{Mental Age}}{\text{Chronological Age}} \times 100 = \text{Intelligence Quotient}$$

The ten-year-old child with a mental age of twelve years has an intelligence quotient of 120, and the ten-year-old child with a mental age of eight years has an intelligence quotient of 80. These procedures provided a scale of comparison which could be used with children of widely different ages. The scale appeared in 1916 and was known as the Stanford-Binet Intelligence Scale. It was soon in common use in America and other English-speaking countries, and was also translated for use in other parts of the world. Indeed it became the best known of all standardized tests of intelligence. Burt (1921), commenting upon the fact that not only were new tests included, but that they also were especially valuable in identifying able children, paid tribute to the Scale as follows: 'Its salient virtue lies in the inclusion of many excellent tests, both fresh and familiar, intended for the higher ages', and also: 'many of the new tests appear to be of much value—particularly those for older and brighter children'.

Terman had therefore a means of identifying children of differing intellectual ability. The opportunity of using it for the selection of highly intelligent children came with the institution, at Stanford University, of a research fellowship for the study of gifted children. Grants of money from other sources in 1921 allowed him considerably to extend his project. There was, however, one other initial problem. He had to decide upon the lower level of ability for inclusion in the research group. He chose an IQ score of 140, taking the view that this would 'insure that subjects admitted to the group would rate within the highest 1 per cent in general intelligence as measured by the tests used' (*The Gifted Child*, 1951).

The investigation which Terman went on to make was very large. There were nearly 700 children in the main experimental group, and over 1,000 in all. The research programme was extensive, detailed and novel, and follow-up studies of many of the children were made throughout the rest of their lives. The study dominated thought and practice on the gifted child in America for many years; in 1962 (*Creativity and Intelligence*), Getzels and Jackson wrote: 'In most studies, the word "gifted" was synonymous with "high IQ" and the term "gifted child" was for all intents and purposes only a shorthand way of saying "child with a high IQ". A child who did not have a high IQ, no matter how accomplished in other respects, was not considered "gifted".'

Although the investigations of the gifted child seem to have been concerned with those children who obtained a high IQ score, the Terman level of 140 was not sacrosanct. There were soon investigations in which a different IQ score was used for selection, although it may be noted that the Stanford-Binet Scale was used almost exclusively. Two examples of studies of children who were selected on a different score can be seen in the work of Professor Leta S. Hollingworth, of Columbia University, New York. In one investigation she studied the characteristics of a small group of children with a Stanford-Binet IQ of 180 or above. In the other investigation in 1922, she arranged special teaching programmes for two separate groups of 26 pupils, both of them attending Public School 165, in New York. In one group all the pupils had a Stanford-Binet score of over 150, and in the other group the scores ranged from 130 to 154.

The individual intelligence test has continued to be the most acceptable method of assessing intellectual ability. It is important to note the changes that have been made in the fifty years since the first Stanford-Binet Scale was developed. The scale itself has twice been revised: in 1937, and again in 1960. The 1937 version sought to assess the intellectual ability of children aged two to fourteen, and also contained groups of tests for those over fourteen. These are known as 'average adult', and 'superior adult' I, II and III. The scale contained two alternative forms, Form L and Form M. The manual to the 1960 scale states: 'It would be safe to say that Form L is used fives times as frequently as Form M' (1960). The most recent scale, the 1960 version, selected the best test items from the two forms of the 1937 version, and combined them into one, the L-M Form.

The early Stanford-Binet Scale (1916), and later its 1937 Revised Version were for many years the most widely used tests. However, a new individual intelligence test for children appeared in 1949. Dr. David Wechsler of the Belle-Vue Psychiatric Hospital, New York, constructed a children's test, the Wechsler Intelligence Scale for Children (WISC), on the pattern of his Wechsler Adult Intelligence Scale. The most important difference from the Binet Scale is the arrangement of the test items into two groups labelled 'Verbal' and 'Performance' respectively. The WISC therefore produces three scores—Verbal,

Performance, and total or Full Scale, as the last-named is called. This test is now widely used in clinical work both in America and in England.

The Stanford-Binet and the Wechsler Scales are both American. Hitherto no similar test has been constructed in England, although forty-seven years ago Sir Cyril Burt stated the need for a native intelligence scale (1921). The gap is likely to be filled in the near future, for a scale, 'The New British Intelligence Scale', is being constructed at the present time under the direction of Professor F. W. Warburton. It is planned to construct a scale to cover the age-range 2-18 years; scores upon a number of specialized abilities will be obtained, and the combined scores may be used as a measure of general mental ability. The scale takes note of recent work on children's thinking, for in addition to the five sub-scales, Reasoning, Verbal, Spatial, Number and Memory, there is a sixth sub-scale, Fluency, which is based upon work on 'creativity'. Some of the items in the sub-scales, such as Number, show the influence of the work of Jean Piaget and others upon the development of logical thinking. 'Creativity' is discussed later in this chapter and in Chapters three and five, and logical thinking is discussed in Chapters four and five.

Ability definitions

The term 'gifted child' is also used to signify a child who shows some specific outstanding ability, as for example, in arithmetic. The child is frequently one who possesses outstanding general intellectual ability, but he may also be a child of high, but not outstandingly high IQ. The ability may be recognized at quite an early age, by an observant parent, teacher or friend who notices an uncommon interest and facility in numbers; it may be revealed by consistently high marks in school work, or by a high score on a standardized achievement test. Certainly the distinctive performance may be seen in the later stages of primary school education and becomes abundantly clear in the secondary school.

A child with outstanding ability in music or painting, dancing or acting, is commonly described as 'gifted' or 'talented'. The abilities required for outstanding performance in these activities do not appear amenable to the same kind of measurement as the abilities possessed by children with a high IQ. It is difficult, if not impossible, to measure the large affective component of artistic performance in the same way. In art, for instance, we are faced with the problem of the assessment of creativity as distinct from the technical capacity to produce art objects. In music we need to distinguish between the level of execution, and the quality of the performance as a whole. Nevertheless, exceptional performance, whether on a specific occasion such as a musical or dramatic performance, or in the creation of a particular work of art, such as a painting or a piece of sculpture, is recognized by those competent to judge. Such outstanding ability attracts the term 'gifted'.

It is possible to continue to isolate areas of human activity, and to consider the individuals who show outstanding ability in those areas as gifted. To the examples given above we may add, for instance, social leadership, mechanical ability, and a wide range of athletic and games skills. This practice leads to statements of the kind expressed in America in the *57th Year Book of the National Society for the Study of Education:* 'The talented or gifted child is one who shows consistently remarkable performance in any worthwhile line of endeavour' (1958).

Creativity

The practice of widening the application of the term 'gifted' may be seen, not only in areas of achievement such as the various modes of artistic performance, but also in some recent efforts to make an assessment of creative thinking abilities.

Some American psychologists have expressed dissatisfaction with the IQ measurement as a means of identifying intellectually gifted children. They consider it has value, but are concerned to draw attention to its limitations. Getzels and Jackson (1962) wrote: 'There is no intent here to derogate the IQ metric as such, for it remains one of the best predictors of academic achievement we have. It "selects in", as it is supposed to do, many students who are likely to achieve better than the average. But at the same time . . . and this is the immediate point . . . it tends to "select out" some students who are also likely to achieve better than average.' The point was also made by Torrance (1962) when he wrote: 'There has been increasing recognition of the fact that traditional measures of intelligence attempt to assess only a few of man's thinking abilities'. There are, it is asserted, other cognitive abilities, concerned with creative thought, which are not measured by the conventional intelligence test, and children who possess these abilities are frequently not recognized. Moreover, these creative thinking abilities are, it is claimed, those which are characteristic of discovery and invention; children who possess these abilities to an extraordinary degree are described as 'gifted'. It is proper to ask the question: 'What are the creative thinking abilities which are not measured by the conventional intelligence test?' Some psychologists and educationists think that part, at least, of the answer is to be found in the studies of intelligence carried out in California by J. P. Guilford.

Guilford (1959) has formed a model of the structure of intelligence, which distinguishes between the 'content' of our thought, the ways in which we think, described as 'operations', and the 'products' of our thought. It can be understood that the form in which thought is held, for example in number, or in words, may be regarded as a different dimension of the intellect than the actual process used in thinking, as for example in remembering or evaluating. Each of these three dimensions of the intellect has sub-divisions: 'contents' has four divisions, 'operations' has five, and 'products' has six. Guilford sees them all as forming an inter-related system ($4 \times 5 \times 6$) providing 120 separate factors or abilities, each of which may be measured. His model of intelligence is shown in the diagram below.

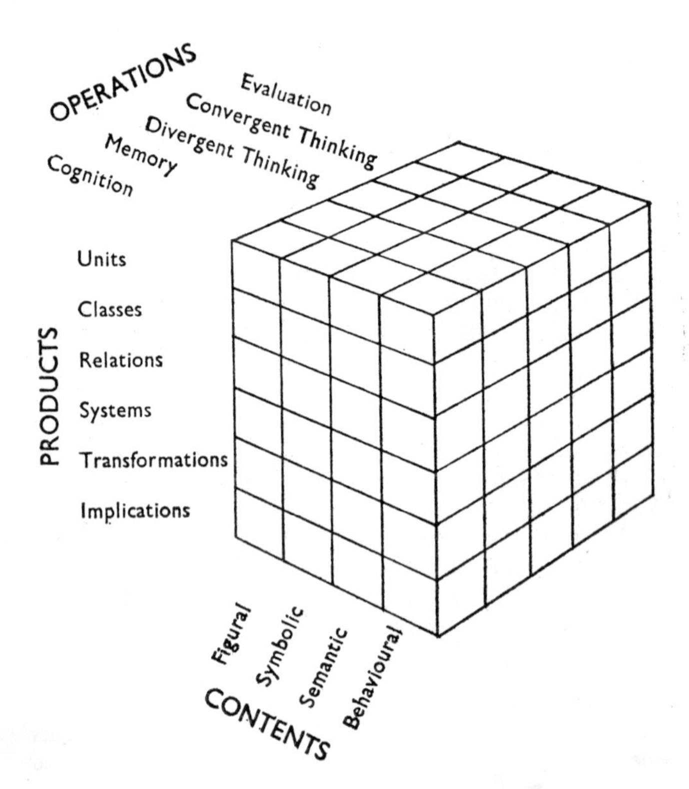

Getzels and Jackson took this new instrument for measuring intelligence into the field of the study of the gifted child. They saw a possible relationship between the categories of convergent and divergent thinking, and the problem of the identification of the gifted child. Therefore they 'undertook to examine empirically the consequences of applying other conceptions of giftedness as well as "high IQ" to the study of children'.

Convergent thinking and divergent thinking are two different modes of thinking which are both categories of Guilford's dimension of 'operations'. The high IQ scorer is good at convergent thinking, for the conventional intelligence test item measures convergent thinking. It asks for data to be handled in such a manner as to provide just one answer, which will commonly be accepted as correct. For example, in the analogy HIGH is to LOW as DRY is to . . . (WET), the correct answer is based upon the perception of relations and the eduction of correlates. Measures of this kind do not, however, necessarily identify all children who possess high abilities. In divergent thinking, thought is considered to proceed in a different manner. It requires the ability to handle data in such a way as to bring forth a variety of responses, each one of which may be acceptable as correct. Subjects may be asked to read an unfinished story, and then complete the story; to use a certain amount of arithmetical data to make up problems; to take a shape, such as a square or a circle, and use it as a base for drawing and elaborating objects and pictures, or to suggest as many uses as possible for a number of common objects, such as a brick or a piece of rope. High level performance in these tests is said to require such characteristics of thought as originality, fluency, flexibility, and the power of elaboration. All of these abilities are commonly regarded as aspects of creative thinking. Some people have argued that creatively-thinking children were not identified by the conventional IQ test. For example, Thurstone (1952) wrote: 'It is a common observation in the universities that those students who have high intelligence judged by available criteria, are not necessarily the ones to produce the most original ideas'. Torrance (1962) wrote: 'This kind of talent (creative thinking) has not been valued and rewarded in our educational system'. It was thinking of this kind which led

Getzels and Jackson to undertake their research in Chicago, in which they asked a number of children to complete a series of tests of divergent thinking. Children who obtained outstandingly high scores were deemed to be highly creative, in fact 'gifted'.

There has been criticism of the use of the terms 'creativity' and 'divergent thinking' as if they were synonymous terms. 'Creativity' is a more comprehensive term, which is used frequently in the primary school. The teacher will speak of 'creative' activities, and this will include creative crafts, creative writing, and creative expression in drama. There are many factors which affect the degree to which the term may be justifiably used at any particular time. However, the essential characteristic of creative work in the junior school is that each child will have the opportunity to create, in words, paint, or movement, construction or arrangement, something which truly springs from himself. It is likely that what he creates will reflect not only his 'knowing' but his 'feeling'; he will express the creativity of the painter or sculptor, as well as the creativity of the engineer or inventor. It is not clear that success in this field reflects the same abilities as are required for successful performance on tests of divergent thinking.

References

BURT, C. (1947). *Mental and Scholastic Tests.* (2nd ed.) London: Staples.

GETZELS, J. P. and JACKSON, P. W. (1962). *Creativity and Intelligence.* London and New York: Wiley.

GUILFORD, J. P. (1959). 'Three faces of intellect', *Amer. Psychologist*, Vol. 14, pp. 469-79.

NATIONAL SOCIETY FOR THE STUDY OF EDUCATION. (1958). *Fifty-seventh Year Book.* Chicago: Public School Publishing Co.

TERMAN, L., *et al.* (1926). *Genetic Studies of Genius*, Vol. I. *Mental and Physical Traits of a Thousand Gifted Children.* (2nd ed.) Stanford, Calif.: Stanford University Press.

TERMAN, L. and ODEN, M. (1951). *The Gifted Child.* (ed. P. WITTY). Boston: Heath, ch. 3.

TERMAN, L. and MERRILL, M. A. (1960). The Stanford-Binet Scale. Boston: Houghton, Mifflin.

THURSTONE, L. L. (1952). 'Creative Talent'. In: THURSTONE, L. L., ed. *Applications of Psychology*. New York: Harper.

TORRANCE, E. P. (1962). *Guiding Creative Talent*. Englewood Cliffs, New Jersey. Prentice-Hall.

WARBURTON, F. W. (1966). 'Construction of the New British Intelligence Scale: progress report', *British Psychological Society Bulletin*, pp. 68-70.

WECHSLER, D. (1949). The Wechsler Intelligence Scale for Children. New York: Psychological Corporation.

Chapter Two

A High IQ

ALMOST all the studies carried out since 1915 have been conducted with children considered to be gifted because they had obtained a high score on a standardized test of intelligence. Three of the major studies we shall look at in this chapter were conducted by Terman in the United States of America (op. cit. 1926), Parkyn in New Zealand (1948), and Burt in England (1962a). After dealing with the structure of these studies an outline is given of a study recently carried out in the north of England by Lovell and Shields, and the findings of all the studies are discussed in this and succeeding chapters.

The investigation directed by Professor Terman was carried out in California between 1921 and 1923. Most of the children lived in urban areas, especially in the larger towns of Los Angeles, San Francisco, Oakland and Berkeley, and were attending the public schools of the state.

Terman had two aims. He wanted to discover the mental and physical traits which were characteristic of the children, and also to study the individual children over as many years as possible. An account of the steps taken to achieve the first aim, and a report of the findings, is described in *The Mental and Physical Traits of a Thousand Gifted Children* (1926).

By a three-stage process of teacher nomination, group intelligence tests, and the Stanford-Binet Intelligence Test, Terman was able to identify a large number of children who met his criterion of being well within the top one per cent in intelligence of the school population. The children were selected if they obtained an IQ score of 140 or more. The final main Experimental Group was very large, and consisted of 643 children (352 boys, and 291 girls) varying in age from 2-13 years; there were 429 children in the age range 8-11 years. Four other groups were studied; a control group, a smaller Binet group, a special ability group, and a high school group.

Terman and his associates then began an inquiry into the abilities, interests and backgrounds of the children. By means of a detailed medical examination, a study of school records, and of performance in a number of tests of educational accomplishments, by home visits, and from statements by parents and teachers, detailed information about each individual was acquired. Parents and teachers were asked to rate the children on a list of twenty-five personality traits.

By the year 1925, Terman had gathered the information he required about the characteristics of the gifted child. He then sought to fulfil the second aim, which was to study the children in adolescence, and in the different stages of adult life. Through his numerous associates he maintained contact with a large number of the subjects right up to his death in 1959. The results of the work are published in three further volumes of the series to which he gave a general title 'Genetic Studies of Genius'; Volume III, *The Promise of Youth* (1930) and Volumes IV and V, written in collaboration with Melita H. Oden, *The Gifted Child Grows Up* (1947), and *The Gifted Group at Mid-Life* (1959).

Parkyn's study was designed to provide information about highly intelligent children in New Zealand. (He used the description 'highly intelligent' rather than 'gifted'.) He described and discussed his findings in the first half of his book published in 1948. He also expressed concern about the education of the highly intelligent child of primary school age, and in the second half of his book he considered questions of school organization, curriculum and teaching methods.

Three groups of children were studied. Groups one and two, although they were made up of intellectually able children, were not at all comparable with Terman's group; they were selected from the records of previously administered group intelligence tests on the basis of scores of 125+, and 120 respectively. Group three, described as 'the Binet group', although small in number, is more comparable. It was made up of 50 pupils (32 boys and 18 girls) in the city of Dunedin, who obtained a score on the Revised Stanford-Binet Scale (1937), which placed them in the top five per cent of their age group. The majority of the children were twelve years old. Information on scholastic performance was obtained from school records and from standardized tests in silent reading, mechanical arithmetic, problem arithmetic, and spelling devised by the Australian Council for Educational Research. Individual interests were studied, homes visited, and an adapted form of the Terman Trait-Rating Questionnaire was completed by the class teacher.

In England, studies similar to those carried out by Terman and Parkyn were carried out by Burt. In 1915 he began the practice of considering the abilities and the performance of the top three per cent of the candidates sitting the London County Council Junior Scholarship Examination, that is to say, children with an IQ score of 128 or more. Information was obtained on school performances, leisure interests, the occupation of parents, and home backgrounds. Burt has reported (1962) that he has maintained contact with many of the subjects, and has collected after-histories for nearly 300 children who obtained IQ scores of 135 or more at the time of the assessment in school.

During the years 1915-62 there appears to have been no other British study of the gifted child in any way comparable with the studies of Terman, Parkyn and Burt. From time to time, notably by Burt (1962), the desirability of such studies has been expressed: 'The problem of the gifted child thus turns out to be unexpectedly complex. Heredity and environment, intelligence and motivation are inextricably involved . . . Facts, however, are still in short supply'.

A study of a group of gifted children living in two cities in the north of England has, however, recently been completed (Lovell and Shields, 1967). All the children, who were between the ages of 8 yrs. 5 ms. and 11 yrs. 7 ms., were identified by a two-stage process of teacher nomination, and by the administration of the Wechsler Intelligence Scale for Children. Verbal, Performance, and Full-Scale IQ's were obtained. Fifty children (35 boys and 15 girls) who obtained Verbal IQ scores of 140 or more, formed the experimental group. The study was designed to obtain current information about the intellectual abilities, language, and personality traits of the gifted child. The following tests were also given:

Divergent Thinking (Creativity) Tests

1. Hidden Shapes (as used by Lovell, 1954, and similar to that used by Getzels and Jackson).

2. Word Association. Subjects were required to give as many different meanings as possible to twenty-five fairly common words, e.g. arm, cap.

3. Uses for Things. Subjects had to write down as many different uses as possible for five common objects, such as a piece of rope.

4. Fables. Four incomplete fables were given. Subjects were asked to compose three different endings for each fable: a moralistic, a humorous, and a sad ending.

5. Make-Up Problems. Three paragraphs were given, each containing many numerical statements describing situations well within the experience of the subjects. They were asked to make up as many problems as they could using the information given.

Tests of Logical Thinking

1. Equilibrium in the Balance (Inhelder and Piaget, 1958).
2. Combinations of Colourless Liquids (Inhelder and Piaget, 1958).
3. The Oscillation of a Pendulum (Inhelder and Piaget, 1958).
4. Concept of Volume (Lovell and Ogilvie, 1961).

Mathematics Tests

1. NFER Number Concept Test. (7+) N.S.44.
2. NFER Concept Arithmetic Test. (10+) N.S.54.
3. NFER Concept Test 'N'.
4. NFER Mathematical Insight Test (14+) N.S.63.
5. A Series and Numerical Analogies Test.
6. Vernon's Graded Arithmetic—Mathematics Test.

Each child also wrote two essays, and a conversation was recorded. In addition the Terman Personality Trait-Rating Form, as used by Terman in his investigation was completed for each child by a teacher who knew him well.

Intellectual abilities

The child with an IQ score of 140 or more will have shown, in his answers to the items of the Stanford-Binet or Wechsler Verbal Intelligence Scales, an overall ability equal to or better than the average child a number of years older than himself. In addition, he may well have shown even more unusual ability in some particular group of tasks. On the other hand, it is very unlikely that he will have approached the average in more than one test item.

High ability and the degree to which it has been used may be perceived in a number of ways. It is likely that the child possesses a fund of general information and knowledge such as could only be gained in the normal day to day processes of education and living, and only retained by a very active and lively mind. Some gifted children may learn lists of historical, geographical and scientific facts for fun, but in general, their intellectual ability and their interests allow them to absorb enormous amounts of information in the most natural manner. Most of the children have extraordinarily keen powers of observation. They will know an object, not only by its total form outline, but by an acute and quick awareness of the minute particulars of its composition. The teacher recognizes this ability when he sees that there are children who not only remember the details to which their attention is drawn, but who notice many details for themselves before the teacher delineates them.

The gifted child frequently excels in the size and quality of his vocabulary. Range and facility of vocabulary are, of course, dependent upon education, experience, reading and conversation. It is also frequently regarded as a good indication of intellectual ability, as may be seen in the remark made by Wechsler (1958): 'Contrary to lay opinion, the size of a man's vocabulary is not only an indication of his schooling, but also an excellent measure of his general intelligence'. Some appreciation of the superiority of the gifted child in the understanding and usage of words may be gained from looking at scores gained on the vocabulary test of the Wechsler Intelligence Scale (op. cit. 1967). One boy aged 9 yrs. 10 ms. scored 56 points. This score is nearly twice as large as the average score of 29-30 points for a child of that age, and is well above the average score of 47-49 points for a young person of 15 yrs. 10 ms. of age. Another boy aged 9 yrs. 2 ms. scored 51 points, nearly twice as many as the 27-28 points gained by the average child of that age, and again a better score than that of the average young person of 15 yrs. 10 ms.

Teachers may be well aware of the pupils who have an extensive vocabulary for they can note it in pupils' written work and in their conversation. It can also be seen that the words are not possessed as lists simply for iteration; rather they are possessed in such an active form as to raise continually the level of discourse. The kind of conversation which a teacher may have with a young gifted child is shown in the following extracts from a conversation which I had with an eight-year-old boy. The passage is not selected to reveal the number of technical or unusual words he may know, but rather to illustrate the general high level of the vocabulary which is at the boy's disposal.

Examiner: Would you care to tell me of some of the things that you are interested in?

John: I *am* interested in astronomy.

Examiner: Well, tell me about it.

John: I've got a book downstairs that tells you about the constellations and the planets. Constellations are groups of stars, and they are named after legendary animals and men . . .
We'll take, for instance, a constellation, Cassiopea . . . There's another one that is supposed to be the king, Cassiopea's the queen—they imagine him to have a beard, looking rather like king Neptune . . . The planets, in order, are Mercury, Venus, Earth, the planet we live on, Mars, Jupiter, Saturn, Uranus, Neptune and Pluto.

Examiner: So Pluto is the furthest.
John: Yes. It was discovered in 1930. Neptune was discovered in 1781 . . . Mercury doesn't have any satellites, that is, celestial bodies circling round it . . .
Examiner: Have you ever looked through a telescope?
John: No.

The gifted child will commonly be distinguished by his power of comprehension. In test situations this is frequently assessed by noting the child's responses to absurd statements. Tansley and Gulliford (1960), describe how an 11-year-old backward child could not deal with the 'verbal absurdities' from the 8-year level of the 1937 Stanford-Binet Scale. The gifted child of 6 or 7 would hoot with laughter at the absurdity, and possibly make a derisory remark about the whole thing. For example: 'They found a young man locked in his room with his hands tied behind him, and his feet bound together. They think he locked himself in'. 'Really, what a stupid thing to say.'

The child who has been declared gifted by reason of a high score on an intelligence test will certainly have shown somewhere in the test that he has a high ability in relational thinking. This ability to see relationships between objects and ideas, and to apply them to new situations, is most important for success in many mental activities. At the same time it is clear that the children in the North of England study who had obtained outstandingly high scores on the Verbal Scale of the Wechsler test (mean IQ 144), did not maintain the very outstanding position in the Performance Scale where the mean IQ was 127.

While the gifted child, no less than the normal or backward child, shows variability in his intellectual abilities, and is more advanced in some areas, less advanced in others, his overall performance in thinking which calls into play the powers of observation, memory, reasoning, relational thinking, and the knowledge and use of words is very high indeed.

Personality traits

Psychologists try to measure personality in a more precise manner than can be done in the normal activities of social and vocational life. Many people would agree with Vernon (1964) when he says that they have not met with much success as yet: 'Psychology seems to be no nearer to providing society with practical techniques which are sufficiently reliable and accurate to win general acceptance'. However, teachers in school continue to make assessments of their pupils (Warburton, 1961, 1962). They will of course in teaching continually react to their own growing awareness of each child's personality, but they are also required in reports and testimonials to make more formal assessments. These are used for the purpose of guidance, especially of children referred to the educational psychologist, for purposes of allocation to a particular kind of school or to a particular class within a school, and for information supplied to employers and to the staffs of institutions of higher education. Some investigations have been made of the value of ratings of personality made by teachers, of the academic performance of their pupils. Warburton (1961) points out that their value may be vitiated by the tendency for the rater's judgement to be affected by his view of the pupil's behaviour in some other trait (the so-called 'halo' effect). A number of studies, however, notably by McClelland (1949), Crane (1959), Astington (1960), and Yates and Pidgeon (1957), have shown that ratings made by primary school teachers of the personality characteristics of their pupils, such as industriousness and perseverance, have predicted success in grammar school work, as well as some of the tests used in secondary school selection procedures. In his article (op. cit., 1962), Warburton goes on to assert the value of personality assessments for research purposes.

The nature of the personality of the gifted child is undoubtedly a matter of great interest to teachers, psychologists, and educational administrators. The biographies and autobiographies of great men and women are a revealing source of information. They may contain, in addition to the life story, fascinating anecdotes, and valuable reflections upon their behaviour when they were children. We should note, however, that these accounts are normally only written by those who have fulfilled the promise of their childhood. But for research evidence on the personality characteristics of the contemporary gifted child, we must go to those who know him well, and especially to his teachers.

The information on personality characteristics which is available from the California, New Zealand, and northern England studies, was obtained very largely from close associates. Using the rating form devised by Terman, 'Ratings on Physical, Mental, Social, and Moral Traits', the teachers, and in the case of Terman's study, the parents also, were asked to rate the children on 25 personality traits. They were to rate in comparison with the average child of the same age, and to use a 13-point scale; Parkyn in fact used only a 9-point scale. The directions given to the rater urged him to be discriminating, and warned him of 'halo' effect.

Terman was able to make statements about the characteristics of the gifted group, not only in relationship to the 'average', but also in terms of their relationship to a control group. He found that the gifted group were rated above average in all traits. Their superiority was very great in general intelligence, originality and commonsense, in the desire to know, the desire to excel, and in a sense of humour; also they showed a rather marked superiority in conscientiousness, truthfulness, self-confidence, will-power and leadership. However, in some traits—fondness for large groups, freedom from vanity and egotism, and in mechanical ingenuity—very little difference was found in comparison with the control group. Mechanical ability was, in fact, placed in the last position, for both boys and girls.

The findings made by Parkyn about the New Zealand children were in general agreement with Terman's findings about the American children, i.e. that they were rated above average in all traits, and the order of superiority of the traits was fairly similar. Some difference did appear between the two groups in those traits classified as 'social traits', for example in fondness for large groups, leadership, and popularity with other children. In these traits the New Zealand children were rated higher than the American. Parkyn suggested that this was possibly due to the more social nature of the schools in New Zealand, which might have permitted teachers to make a more accurate assessment of pupils' 'social traits'. It is also interesting to note that 'mechanical ingenuity' was placed in the twenty-fifth position for the girls in New Zealand as it was in America, but in the ratings for the boys it had risen to the sixteenth position. Here again Parkyn thought that the social nature of the New Zealand schools had made possible a more accurate assessment.

These findings on the personality traits of the gifted child were the result of studies carried out in countries far distant from Britain. Information about the personality characteristics of gifted children in England can be obtained from Burt's studies, and from the recent inquiry in the north of England.

Burt, too, found that the gifted children were in all traits almost always ahead of other children of the same chronological age. In addition, he reported that he found very few examples of children with severe behavioural difficulties. He did, however, declare that in an environment unfavourable to the satisfaction of intellectual qualities, the superiority of social and moral traits was not so strong as it was among pupils with a favourable environment.

In the more recent study in two cities in the north of England, the findings are very similar to those of the earlier studies. Terman's trait-rating form was used on a scale from 1—13 points, with the lower scores denoting stronger possession of the traits.

TABLE 1

RANK ORDER	TRAIT	MEAN
1.	General Intelligence	2·40
2.	Desire to Know	2·48
3.	Originality	3·26
4.	Desire to Excel	3·44
5.	Truthfulness	3·68
6.	Commonsense	3·82
7.5	Will-power and Perseverance	3·88
7.5	Conscientiousness	3·88
9.	Prudence and Forethought	4·30
10.	Self-Confidence	4·54
11.	Sense of Humour	4·96
12.	Cheerfulness and Optimism	5·00
13.	Amount of Physical Energy	5·04
14.5	Health	5·22
14.5	Sensitiveness to Approval and Disapproval	5·22
16.	Permanency of Moods	5·36
17.	Generosity and Unselfishness	5·40
18.	Appreciation of Beauty	5·60
19.	Sympathy and Tenderness	5·82
20.5	Fondness for Large Groups	5·86
20.5	Popularity with Other Children	5·86
22.	Musical Appreciation	5·96
23.	Mechanical Ingenuity	5·98
24.	Leadership	6·00
25.	Freedom from Vanity and Egotism	6·14

It can be seen from the table that the Personality ratings varied from a mean rating of 2·4 for General Intelligence to 6·14 for Freedom from Vanity and Egotism. The means of all the ratings were therefore less than 7, and we may say that, in the opinion of the teachers, these gifted children were above average on all the traits. They were rated as outstandingly high in General Intelligence and Desire to Know; very high in Originality, Desire to Excel, Truthfulness, Commonsense Will-power and Perseverance, and Conscientiousness; rather high in Prudence and Forethought, Self-confidence and Sense of Humour. In a few traits they were rated close to average, and the poorest rating was obtained for Freedom from Vanity and Egotism. There were a few differences between the boys and girls. Boys were rated somewhat higher on Sensitiveness to Approval or Disapproval, Amount of Physical Energy,

Fondness for Large Groups and Mechanical Ingenuity; whereas girls were rated rather higher for Appreciation of Beauty, Musical Appreciation and Freedom from Vanity and Egotism.

There was close agreement with Terman in the order of the traits. Table 2 shows the rank order of the traits in the two studies carried out in California and northern England.

TABLE 2

TRAIT	RANK ORDER America	RANK ORDER North of England
1. Health	15	14.5
2. Amount of Physical Energy	20	13
3. Prudence and Forethought	12	9
4. Self-confidence	9	10
5. Will-power and Perseverance	5	7.5
6. Musical Appreciation	17	22
7. Appreciation of Beauty	16	18
8. Sense of Humour	11	11
9. Cheerfulness and Optimism	10	12
10. Permanency of Moods	13	16
11. Fondness for Large Groups	22	20.5
12. Leadership	24	24
13. Popularity with Other Children	23	20.5
14. Sensitivity to Approval and Disapproval	19	14.5
15. Desire to Excel	3	4
16. Freedom from Vanity and Egotism	18	25
17. Sympathy and Tenderness	14	19
18. Generosity and Unselfishness	21	17
19. Conscientiousness	7	7.5
20. Truthfulness	6	5
21. Mechanical Ingenuity	25	23
22. Desire to Know	2	2
23. Originality	8	3
24. Commonsense	4	6
25. General Intelligence	1	1

It can be seen from the table that in the case of no less than fourteen of the traits rated by the two groups of teachers, the order in which they are regarded as superior to the average is within two places of one another: Desire to Know is placed second in both studies, Sense of Humour is placed eleventh in both studies, Cheerfulness and Optimism is placed tenth in one list and twelfth in the other. In only two traits, Amount of Physical Energy and Freedom from Vanity and Egotism is there a difference of a magnitude as high as seven places. The Spearman Rank Difference Correlation Coefficient for the two groups was +·90. It may be noted also that Terman classified the traits as intellectual, volitional, emotional, moral, social and physical, and wrote: '. . . one can say with considerable assurance that gifted children excel the average most of all in intellectual and volitional traits, next in emotional and moral traits, and least in physical and social traits'.

When the ratings made by the teachers in the recent English study are similarly classified, apart from a change in position between emotional and moral traits the results are identical, the order being, intellectual, volitional, moral, emotional, physical and social. If we note that one study is a contemporary study of a relatively small number of children in two northern cities of England, and the other is a study of a much larger number of children in California more than forty years ago, the degree of agreement of the findings is quite remarkable. Evidently, despite changes in education and life in the United States of America and the United Kingdom from 1920 to 1960, the gifted child seems to his teacher to be much the same kind of person.

Lovell and Shields (1967) say that their results suggest that gifted children in general could be said to show the following characteristics. They possess, in addition to their high intelligence, strong drives to do well; they are healthy, energetic, cheerful, sociable, popular and regarded as leaders. They are inventive, possess commonsense, an eye for beauty and a stable temperament; they show a sense of humour and a sense of modesty. They are sympathetic, generous, conscientious and truthful, and also show qualities of prudence and perseverance.

Physical characteristics

There seems little doubt that the highly intelligent child cannot be considered in any way inferior in physical attributes and accomplishments. It is true that his physical traits, in relation to the general standard of pupils of equal age, in no way match his outstanding intellectual abilities; assessments of physical traits have, however, shown him to be slightly above average.

Terman (op. cit. 1926), devotes three quite long chapters to a detailed account of the various measurements made of the physical condition of his gifted children. Thirty-seven measurements were made, including measurements of height, weight, arm span, and length of leg. Medical history records were built up from information supplied by parents and schools, and each child was medically examined by two physicians. A picture of good health was presented. The children were above average in height and weight; they exceeded the children of a control group in physical measurements such as length of arm span and width of shoulders; there were fewer children with defective vision than in the control group; and there were fewer reports of headaches and general weakness. The doctors conducting the medical examination agreed that physically the children were superior to unselected children of corresponding age in the school population, and over all they were impressed by their general sense of well-being. Parkyn reported that in the measurements made of the children in his study, the median height of the highly intelligent group living in Dunedin was two inches above the New Zealand average, and the median weight was eleven pounds above the average.

We may well add to these findings the opinion of the teachers. Terman compiled a Personality Trait Rating Form in which he asked the teachers to rate the children on 25 personality traits in relation to the average child of the same age. The Californian teachers using a 13-point scale gave above average ratings for Health at 5·9 for boys and 5·3 for girls, and also above average for Amount of

Physical Energy at 6·1 for boys and 5·5 for girls. Using the same rating scale, the teachers in the north of England study recently gave ratings, for boys and girls combined, of 5·2 for Health and 5·0 for Amount of Physical Energy. The results in New Zealand using the same form, but with only a 9-point scale, were of a similar nature. Burt also reported that the gifted children were above average in physical characteristics.

It may be said, in summary, that forty years ago, Terman felt that he had evidence to show that the gifted child was above average in physical traits, and that he could clearly refute the view, apparently held at the time, that 'typically the intellectually precocious child is weak, undersized, or nervously unstable'. We may also say that subsequent investigations have corroborated his findings.

There is, however, need to give a warning about the inferences to be made from the association of high intellectual ability and physical development. The good physical development may be due to environmental factors. In all the studies reported, the majority of the children had parents who were engaged in professional or highly skilled occupations. These parents tend to provide those things which are conducive to good physical development, for example, regular and good meals, and regular and sufficient hours of sleep. Terman himself felt that the slight superiority of his gifted group might be due to diet and medical care. Burt made the same point. He reported (op. cit. 1962) that the findings about the physical characteristics of the children he studied were similar to those of Terman, but he felt that much of the physical superiority might be 'accounted for by differences in the material conditions of the different social classes at the time of the inquiry'. More recently Tanner (1961) has reported the physical superiority today of children of parents in professional occupations: 'The difference in height between children of the professional and managerial classes and those of unskilled labourers is currently about an inch at 3 years, rising to 1½ or even 2 inches at adolescence'. And: 'In weight the difference is relatively less (from 1 lb. to 8 lb. in most data)'. However, Tanner had also discussed the role of hereditary factors in the control of growth, and suggested that, 'genetical control evidently operates throughout the whole process of growth'.

In the same work, Tanner (1961) discussed in some detail the question of the relationship between physical maturation and mental ability. He cited a number of research findings in America, England and Scotland which led him to say: 'Children who are physically advanced for their age do, in fact, score higher in mental ability tests than those who are less mature, but of the same chronological age'. Douglas (1964) in *The Home and the School*, a report of a study which covered the whole range of intellectual ability, found that girls who reached puberty earlier were superior in measured intellectual ability. He did not, however, ascribe the intellectual superiority to greater physical maturation. He thought that the explanation was to be found in the fact that many of the children were only children, or came from families with few children. Douglas also reports that there are studies which 'suggest that from the age of seventeen onwards the late developers catch up and that by the time of entry to the University they are academically more successful than the early developers'. A recent study reported by Nisbet, *et al.* (1964) also indicates that the differences in intellectual ability between the earlier and late maturing girl are considerably less at the age of sixteen.

In summary, it would seem that we may expect the more intelligent child to be somewhat advanced in physical development. We should note, however, Tanner's statement: 'We do not know whether this relation between intelligence and size reflects a genetical effect on both, or whether both superior weight and intelligence come from excellence of child care'. The evidence on the gifted child which is available, comes from medical examinations which were conducted forty years ago, and from teacher ratings which are not very precise and have no pretentions to medical authority. Evidence which is contemporary and expert is required, and could be gained from at least three sources: the school medical examination records of children who made outstanding scores at the time of the secondary school examination; the large-scale growth and development studies now in progress; and future investigations of the gifted child.

Academic achievements

Many people take an interest in observing the use which is made of ability. It is particularly interesting to see how the gifted child is getting on with basic school subjects, and, as he grows older, to what degree he is acquiring the scientific and social concepts which are the tools of the educated man.

The American children performed far above the level of the average pupil. Their academic achievement was measured by the use of the Stanford Achievement Tests in reading, arithmetic, language usage, and in spelling, and also by an extensive general information test. An accomplishment quotient calculated from the pupils' performance on the Stanford Achievement Tests produced an average score of 144. (The average intelligence quotient for the group was 151.) The academic performance of the pupils was therefore equal to that achieved by the average pupil who was three or four years older; it was, however, not quite so outstanding as the performance in the Stanford-Binet Intelligence Test.

The children in New Zealand completed a series of tests in English, reading, word knowledge, and spelling, and they also completed a number of tests of mechanical and problem arithmetic. The tests were compiled by the Australian Council for Educational Research, and were taken at the same time by approximately 700 other children. Parkyn reported that the 'Binet group' of children occupied thirty-five per cent of the top places in these tests of attainment.

The pupils in the recent English study were asked to complete only one standardized test of achievement—Vernon's Graded Arithmetic-Mathematics Test. They acquitted themselves very well. The mean achievement age was 3 yrs. 7 ms. in advance of the mean chronological age; twelve pupils were from 4 to 5 years in advance of their chronological age, three were 5 years or more in advance, and one pupil, Brian, aged 10 yrs. 5 ms., equalled the score of the average pupil of 16 yrs. 2 ms.

When considering the relationship between intelligence test scores and performance on scholastic achievement tests, it would be absurd to expect all the children with the highest intelligence test scores to achieve the highest scholastic performance. General intellectual ability is a factor which consistently correlates well with academic performance; there are, however, other factors which affect performance, such as motivation, special abilities and disabilities (Burt, 1962), and health. Parkyn felt that many of the instances in which performance in the achievement tests of the highly intelligent group was exceeded by pupils with lower IQ scores, could be explained by the presence of special abilities. However, he was also of the opinion that after due allowance for the various factors which might affect performance had been made, the achievement scores of the 'Binet group' were low in relation to measured ability.

It is a truism to say that ability and desire are twin requisites for the achievement of a high standard of learning. Opportunity is a third factor of considerable importance. Opportunities for learning occur in many places; the school, however, is the institution which exists to provide opportunities for children to learn, arising from the skill of the teacher, the facilities provided, the curriculum which is followed, and the teaching methods which are employed. The opportunities given in the class of the first year may well be different from those given in a class of the second year, and certainly the average 10-year-old pupil will experience opportunities which are different from those available to the average 8-year-old.

The earlier investigators showed considerable interest in the actual grade or class to which gifted pupils were assigned. Terman found that by far the greater number of his pupils (85 per cent) were accelerated in grade placement. However, by the use of a school progress quotient, analogous to an intelligence quotient, and to an educational quotient, he calculated that the average grade placement was only 14 per cent above the norm. He was moved to comment: 'It is evidently a rare experience for a gifted child to be given work of a grade of difficulty commensurate with his intellectual abilities'. Parkyn's highly intelligent group in New Zealand was accelerated by half a year. The average progress quotients were 105 for the boys and 103 for the girls. Burt reported an average progress quotient of 118 for the London schoolchildren. The question of allocation of pupils to particular classes, or indeed to particular schools, must of course be related to the broader educational aims of society at large, of particular schools, and of the individual class.

The standardized test of achievement is not the only means of assessing a child's academic knowledge. Conversation can reveal not only the specific facts which have been learnt, but the extent to which they are available for use. Consider this extract from a conversation with a boy of 10. There was no interview or simulated examination preparation. The boy came from his classroom on the last day of the summer term, and sat down in a small room, and we talked together for a little while.

Michael: I suppose that my main hobby is archaeology . . . it's the study of ancient people . . . and history . . . in which you dig up remains.

Examiner: Have you done any digging yourself?

Michael: Yes, quite a bit. I've found quite a few bits of pottery.

Examiner: Which century pottery did you say it was?

Michael: I've found a few bits of sixteenth century . . . and at quite a deep level, although I would say they were eighteenth century or later, I've found some nice jars.

Examiner: Which books have you read about archaeology?

Michael: I generally read the ones about ancient Egypt and ancient Greece; I'm interested in those two civilizations.

Examiner: Can you tell me a little about them?

Michael: Egypt was the older, starting with the beginning of the dynastic period in 3200 BC approx. . . . and they worshipped gods fairly similar to the Greek ones, except with different names . . . and slightly different aspects. The proper Greeks started much later in about 800 BC, but before that comes the civilization known as the Mycenean, or Minoan, or Cretan, or whatever you like to call them.

Examiner: The proper Greeks? Do you mean on the mainland?

Michael: Yes.

Examiner: And which cities would you say became the most famous of the Greeks?

Michael: Well . . . Athens . . . Delphi . . . Delphi was really an oracle place . . . Corinth . . . Sparta . . . such places.

Examiner: Can you tell me the names of any of the famous Athenians?

Michael: Socrates . . . Plato . . . Pericles . . .

Examiner: What sort of men would we say they were?

Michael: Most of them philosophers.

Examiner: What is a philosopher, Michael?

Michael: Well . . . personally I've never really understood philosophy myself (chuckles from both) . . . a person who says . . . what is? what is? . . . what is what? . . .

Examiner: Do you go to the theatre very much?
Michael: Well, I write my own plays generally. We have a little acting club, me and my friends . . .

Leisure pursuits

At school, children follow an educational programme which is prescribed for them by their teachers; a menu table d'hôte rather than à la carte. But there is more to living and learning than school provides. There are the hours of winter darkness, and of summer light; there are the holidays from school.

What are the interests and activities which absorb the energies and free time of gifted children?

The children are tremendous readers. They start early—nearly half of Terman's gifted learnt to read before starting school. Some were reported as reading before the age of three. Many of them, moreover, learnt to read with little or no formal instruction. While time showed that some children were attracted to practical activities at least as much as to reading, an apposite comment upon the gifted child would be, 'Frequently to be seen with his nose in a book'. Terman wrote: 'The typical gifted child of seven years reads more books than the unselected child reads at any age up to fifteen years'.

Making a similar observation about the children in Dunedin, Parkyn wrote: 'In no activity more than in reading do we find such a difference between these children and the average twelve- or thirteen-year-old.' These children appear to take pleasure in revealing their love of reading, almost as if they are savouring both past and future delights. Comments taken from the conversations with the children in the north of England study, exemplify the children's feelings.

'Yes, I like reading.'

'Well, one of my favourite hobbies is reading. I've got a load of well-known books.'

'I do like reading. I do most of it in bed. I read a book or two a night.'
'Books, all sorts.'

Quantity of reading is indicative; so is content.

Burt wrote that the younger children 'would read almost anything that came their way' (op. cit. 1962). Parkyn (1948) reported that of all his pupils, they (the Binet 50) 'read anything and everything that comes their way'. In their reading of non-fictional books gifted children favour encyclopaedias and other books of general information. But as they reach nine or ten years of age there is, in their choice of books, a reflection of their developing special interests, historical, geographical, or scientific; this point is illustrated by the following quotations:

'I like science and science fiction. The ones I have at the moment are chemistry.' (This boy, Charles, aged nine is intent on being a student of chemistry.) And . . . ' "Everyday Machines" ' . . . how things work, how keys work, cylinder locks, and bank vault locks. How washing machines work, and irons, and electric light bulbs, and fluorescent bulbs . . .'

And another boy:

'I like reading geography books. I've got some from the library at the moment, *Young Travellers in Norway*. I've tried to collect nearly all the series on Travellers . . .

As in the case of non-fiction reading, certain predilections appear in their choice of books of fiction.

A girl of ten years said:

'I like reading thrillers, and "who-dun-its". Agatha Christie . . . she's my favourite, and of the others I just read anyone I can find.'

And a boy:

'Adventure books, mostly war stories if I can.'

Among the gifted there are few idle hands. Hobbies and pastimes, as well as reading, loom large in their lives. Burt (1962) reported that the gifted child in London was almost as well distinguished by the number and nature of his hobbies and pastimes as he was by the amount and quality of his reading. He also showed how the boys, in particular, were distinguished by their scientific interests and constructional activities; they frequently carried out experiments and frequently made working models. Parkyn (1948) also commented upon 'the variety and scope' of the hobbies, and showed how within a year or two many were highly specialized and showed great technical efficiency. He wrote: 'The versatility of the children was amazing, and the competence in planning and the precision in execution wholly admirable'.

Terman's gifted do not appear to have shown the same distinctive interest in practical pursuits as in literary ones. Questions from which numerical data might be gained on this point were not put in the recent English study, but the impression gained from talking to the children supports Burt and Parkyn, rather than Terman. The range of interests and pastimes of some of the children was really quite extraordinary. One ten-year-old boy, Harry, spoke as follows: 'I like going swimming to the public baths . . . I also like doing model kits, and did two three-shilling-scale figures a few days ago—Julius Caesar and Richard the First, Richard the Lionheart. My brother likes fishing, but I'm not terribly keen. I like music . . . I like pieces by Tchaikovsky, he's my favourite music composer. I do like bits of pop music. I like Cliff Richard, the Shadows, and the Beatles. I play two instruments, the violin and the piano . . . I'm a choirboy. I used to be in the Cubs, but now I've got the problem of which shall I join . . . the Scouts . . . or what. I want to join the Boys Club. Well, I am a member, but I want to stay in that. It's in the Church

Hall; there's games, table tennis, snooker, billiards, darts . . . I like athletics and boxing. I've got a pair of boxing gloves; we used to have a punch bag, it was an old settee mat, but it was nearly as good.'

'Are you interested in Nature Study?'

'Yes, I go on nature walks. I go down by the river. There are a lot of interesting things you can find . . . I like looking for flowers especially, leaves . . . and we keep a book. We flat them, and stick them in and tell about them . . . the day found . . . I haven't had anything new since December 20th, I think. Oh, I saw a jay and a 20 inch long rook.'

'How did you know it was 20 inches long?'

'Well, we could see from the length of it, and most of them are about 18 inches long; well, it was more than 20, it was about 22. You can tell it was because there was another by it, and the other one you see was normal size. I like stamp collecting. I also like doing things for model trains; we've got one, but it's not a very good one unfortunately.'

'Tell me a little about the Model Exhibition you went to see the other day.'

'It was very crowded. There was one which I rather liked; there was a little mine which came out to a mains circuit; at the other end of the circuit was a large shunting yard. There was another one with a very good idea, in Airfix . . .'

'Do you like going to the theatre?'

'Yes, I go occasionally. I go quite often to the cinema; we might be going this afternoon. I want to see "Spartacus". I love Sparta and the Greeks. I especially like Alexander the Great, I think he's fabulous. We had a story about him. She (the teacher) has told us recently that the five greatest generals in all times were, in this order, Alexander the Great . . . what was the other chap? . . . there was a chap who beat Hannibal . . . and there's Hannibal, and Julius Caesar, and Napoleon, and . . . Publius Scipio, that's it. When I grow up, if I have a boy, I would like to call him Alexander.'

'You didn't include the Duke of Wellington.'

'No, well . . . that is . . . there's no British in it.'
'Field-Marshall Montgomery?'
'Well, I'm Welsh, anyway.'

Terman was struck by the interest shown in making collections, especially those of a scientific nature. Burt, in speaking of the frequency of scientific hobbies, referred to collections of stamps, fossils, and the like. On the other hand, while Parkyn instanced stamp collecting as a hobby, he did not report that the pupils were particularly characterized by the practice of making collections. But there were certainly examples of many collections made by the children in the recent study in the north of England. One boy, Andrew, aged ten told me this:

> 'I've got about two-thousand foreign stamps . . . and a box of about four-hundred Brooke Bond Tea Cards . . . Bird Portraits, British Wild Life, Fresh Water Fish. When I . . . I am going to start a museum. I brought some stone from Cumberland, and I know where I can get some granite and some limestone, and some sandstone, and so on. . . . There's my friends, Leslie's keen on birds' eggs, Paul's keen on birds, and I'm mainly keen on the wild life that crawls and flies, meaning entomology, ornithology, and lepidopterae . . .'

Another boy, David, aged nine said:

> 'I've got my own sort of little museum thing . . . it's nothing very much. It's just a collection of all the interesting rocks and fossils that I've found. There's a lot of ammonites in it, and also a lot of types of crystals in it. We started a society called the Society of Geology, and we've made a little school museum.'

A girl, Sara, aged nine, almost whispered:

> 'I've a collection of dolls . . . sometimes if I've nothing to do, I stand outside the case that they're in, and I pretend that they're talking.'
> 'Do they talk aloud?'
> 'Sometimes I make them.'

References

ASTINGTON, E. (1960). 'Personality assessment and performance in a boys' grammar school', *Brit. J. Educ. Psychol.*, 30, pp. 225-36.

BURT, C. (1962a). 'General introduction: the gifted child'. In: BEREDAY, G. Z. F. and LAUWERYS, J. A., eds. *The Year Book of Education, 1962.* London: Evans; pp. 24-58.

BURT, C. (1962b). 'The gifted child', *Times Educational Supplement*, 26 Jan.

CRANE, G. (1959). 'The value of persistence in selection for secondary education', *Brit. J. Educ. Psychol.* 29, pp. 77-8.

DOUGLAS, J. W. B. (1964). *The Home and the School.* London: MacGibbon & Kee.

GETZELS, J. W. and JACKSON, P. W. (1962). *Creativity and Intelligence.* London and New York: Wiley.

INHELDER, B. and PIAGET, J. (1958). *The Growth of Logical Thinking from Childhood to Adolescence.* London: Routledge & Kegan Paul.

LOVELL, K. and OGILVIE, E. (1961). 'The growth of the concept of volume in junior school children', *J. Child. Psychol. Psychiat.*, Vol. 2, pp. 118-26.

LOVELL, K. and SHIELDS, J. B. (1967). 'Some aspects of a study of the gifted child', *Brit. J. Educ. Psychol.*, 37, pp. 201-8.

MCCLELLAND. (1949). *Selection for University Education.* London: Univ. of London Press; quoted by WARBURTON, F. W. (1961). 'The measurement of personality—I', *Educ. Res.*, Vol. 4, No. 1, pp. 2-17.

NISBET, J. D., *et al.* (1964). 'Puberty and test performance: a further report', *Brit. J. Educ. Psychol.*, 34, pp. 202-3.

PARKYN, G. W. (1948). *Children of High Intelligence. A New Zealand Study.* New Zealand Council for Educational Research. London: Oxford University Press.

TANNER, A. E. and GULLIFORD, R. (1960). *The Education of Slow Learning Children.* London: Routledge & Kegan Paul.

TANNER, J. M. (1961). *Education and Physical Growth.* London: University of London Press.

TERMAN, L., *et al.* (1926). *Genetic Studies of Genius, Vol.* 1*: Mental and Physical Traits of a Thousand Gifted Children.* (2nd ed.) Stanford Calif: Stanford University Press.

VERNON, P. E. (1964). *Personality Assessment.* London: Methuen.

WARBURTON, F. W. (1961). 'The measurement of personality—I', *Educ. Res.*, Vol. IV, No. 1, pp. 2-17.

WECHSLER, D. (1958). *The Measurement and Appraisal of Adult Intelligence.* (4th ed.) Baltimore: Williams & Wilkins.

YATES, A. E. and PIDGEON, D. (1957). *Admission to Grammar Schools.* NFER Publications, No. 10. London: Newnes Educational. (For NFER).

Chapter Three

Creativity

RESEARCH studies of gifted children have usually been conducted with children who obtained a high score on an individual intelligence test, either the Stanford-Binet Intelligence Scale or the Wechsler Intelligence Scale for Children.

Another procedure to identify gifted children for research purposes selects children on the basis of a high score on a number of tests of 'divergent thinking'.

Tests of divergent thinking, which are also described as 'creativity tests', have aroused a great deal of interest and activity in America, and some interest and activity in Britain. Although the form in which the tests appear is new, the sudden upsurge of interest and work on tests which seek to measure productive abilities of thought is a resurgence rather than an innovation. Professors Getzel and Jackson (op. cit. 1962) refer to American work extending as far back as 1906, and Professor Sir Cyril Burt (op. cit. 1962a), shows that work of this kind was not confined to America, but occurred in Britain, in the earlier years of this century.

Although there is conflict in the findings of the various recent research studies on creativity, there are sound reasons why a knowledge of the studies is interesting and valuable.

Creativity has long been a subject of great interest to mankind, and there is to-day considerable interest in its nature, and in the possible modes of its origin and development. *The Act of Creation* by A. Koestler (1964), is written upon this very issue. There is also interest in many areas of society, such as industry, in the development and use of each individual's creative abilities. This interest is shown in the complex work of advanced industrial research and design, and in the works suggestion box, with the associated special monetary rewards for ideas which prove to be of value. It is also shown in the vast range of creative activities and creative teaching procedures currently advocated and employed with children of all ages, and in all subjects of the school curriculum, in the arts, sciences, and crafts, and in physical education.

Great men are frequently regarded as such because they have shown that they possess extraordinary creative powers. Galton (1869) in his book *Hereditary Genius* gives a list of qualities, for which he declares, the world 'almost unconsciously allots marks to men'; the first quality which he names is 'originality of conception'. It is also illuminating to examine the responses made by children to the tests of divergent thinking. It is possible that part of the benefit of the inquiries into creativity will be in the help that they give to teachers in the planning of their own teaching procedures.

Divergent thinking

It was reported in chapter two that the work on creativity stemmed from the distinction made by Guilford between convergent and divergent thinking. Convergent thinking was said to involve the kind of thinking which is required for the correct solution of the tasks which are set in the conventional intelligence test. Divergent thinking was characterized by originality, fluency, and flexibility of thought, and also by an ability to elaborate; this was productive, rather than reproductive thinking. Tests constructed to measure these abilities would therefore be measuring the power and flow of invention and imagination, i.e. creative thinking abilities. It was also reported in chapter two that Getzels and Jackson saw a possible relationship between convergent and divergent thinking and the problem of identifying the gifted child. They considered that the practice of using IQ as the sole measure of intellectual giftedness led to the undervaluing of other intellectual abilities; in particular, they felt that creative thinking abilities were seriously undervalued at all educational levels in the United States. Therefore they 'undertook to examine empirically the consequences of applying other conceptions of giftedness as well as "high IQ" to the study of children'. They found this 'other conception of giftedness' in the proposition that divergent thinking was indeed a different mode of thinking from convergent thinking, and that the pupils who achieved an outstanding score in tests of divergent thinking could be regarded as gifted in the underlying abilities, which were creative thinking abilities.

Creativity and intelligence

To test the proposition, Getzels and Jackson tested 292 boys and 241 girls aged between 12 and 17 years who were attending a high school in Chicago, and obtained from them scores on a number of creativity tests, and on a number of scholastic achievement tests. The school supplied intelligence test scores for the pupils, and the mean score was 132.

The scores obtained by the pupils in the intelligence, creativity, and scholastic achievement tests were examined, and as a result, Getzels and Jackson felt that they had evidence to suggest that at the 'high average level of intelligence and above, IQ and creativity are sufficiently independent to warrant differentiation' (op. cit. 1962, p. 26).

They based this finding upon two points arising from the investigation. First, they examined the inter-relationship of the scores which were obtained in the IQ tests and in the creativity tests by the total experimental group; the scores can be seen on page 20 of their book, *Creativity and Intelligence*. They make the point that the relationship between the scores on each of the creativity tests and the scores obtained on the IQ test is low; in point of fact no correlation reaches the figure of 0·4. Second, from the scores of the total group, they identified two small groups of pupils who differed in the following manner: 'one high in intelligence but not concomitantly high in creativity, the other high in creativity, but not concomitantly high in intelligence' (op. cit. p. 16). When the scores obtained by these two groups of pupils in the tests of scholastic achievement were compared, it was found that the high creativity group (mean IQ 127) had scored higher than the high IQ group (mean IQ 150), in spite of the fact that the average IQ score was lower by 23 points. This is shown in the following table:

TABLE 3 (EXTRACT): MEAN SCHOOL ACHIEVEMENT SCORES

TOTAL POPULATION (N=449)	HIGH IQ GROUP (N=28)	HIGH CREATIVITY GROUP (N=24)
49·91	55·00	56·27

Clearly the 'highly creative' group had performed far better in the achievement tests than was to be expected from their IQ scores.

There are, of course, factors other than general intelligence which can affect performance in achievement tests. Getzels and Jackson considered initially that the difference in the scores from the two groups might be due to motivational factors. They used two tests to measure the 'need for achievement' of the two groups, and found that the two groups 'differed neither from each other, nor from the total experimental group'. They therefore rejected the proposition that motivational factors were responsible for the surprisingly high scholastic achievement of the 'highly creative' group. They returned to the thesis that there existed divergent thinking or creative abilities which were independent of the cognitive abilities measured by IQ tests, and asserted their belief that the creatively gifted group did indeed have at their disposal cognitive abilities which were not measured by the conventional IQ test, and that these abilities were in part responsible for the high scores which the group had obtained in the scholastic achievement tests.

There have been a number of criticisms of the investigation by Burt (1962), Vernon (1964), Marsh (1964), Yamamoto (1965), Wallach and Kogan (1965), and Cropley (1966). Some of the criticisms are concerned with the procedures by which the data was obtained, and some are concerned with the interpretation of the data.

The IQ scores were obtained from school records, and the same test was not used for all pupils, so it is felt that their reliability may not be very high. Doubt can also be held about the reliability of the creativity tests themselves, because no evidence was given of scores obtained when the tests had been tried with other groups of pupils. Further, there was no evidence to suggest what the relationship was between these tests and performance in 'creative' activities in adult life.

With regard to the interpretation of the data, Burt (op. cit. 1962a), took the view that the claim that creative thinking abilities existed independently of IQ was not justified. The claim had been made partly on the basis of a low relationship between the scores obtained on the IQ tests and the scores obtained on the creativity tests, but, as Burt pointed out (op. cit. 1962a, p. 295), the relationship between the scores obtained on the separate tests of creativity themselves was very little higher. It is just as logical to regard these tests as similarly independent of one another. This point of the low inter-relationship of the creativity tests was also made by Hudson (1964); he reported similar results from his own studies in England, although he preferred to describe the tests as 'open-ended' tests.

Wallach and Kogan (1965) also commented upon the lack of internal consistency among the set of creativity measures, and, like Burt, could not accept that there was sufficient evidence to justify the assertion of a domain of creative thinking abilities which existed independent of the intellectual abilities which were measured by the conventional test of intelligence. Further, it may be noted that Vernon (1964) pointed out that psychometrists, other than Guilford's own followers, had not generally confirmed the enormous number of distinct factors which he claimed. In support of this Vernon cited Sultan's (1962) research in London with second-year grammar school boys; in this investigation it was found that Guilford's 'creativity' factors tended to break up into familiar factors such as general, verbal, spatial ability, and fluency, the only creativity factor emerging being a small 'originality' one. If the evidence for Guilford's factors is not strong, this must, of course, reflect on Getzels and Jackson's thesis. It is therefore interesting to see that the recent work of Harris and Liba (1965) has thrown some doubt on the validity of Guilford's model of the structure of the intellect.

However, even among the writers who do not accept Professors Getzels and Jackson's rather large claim for creative abilities independent of IQ, there is some acceptance of the proposition that creative thinking abilities exist, and that they may be measured by tests of the kind used by Getzels and Jackson. Burt wrote: 'These new tests have succeeded in eliciting supplementary activities that are rarely tapped by the usual brands of intelligence tests' (op. cit. 1962, p. 295). If this view is accepted, it may well be reasonable to speak of a child who is 'creatively' gifted, as we speak of a child who is gifted in some special area, as in, for example, mathematics. Burt had indeed reported earlier (1949, 1962) that his own research indicated the existence of a special creative ability.

The pupils studied by Getzels and Jackson, and also by Hudson, were aged 12-17 years and therefore somewhat older than the children written about in chapter two, who were between the ages of 8 years and 12 years. It is interesting to look at a study of the relationship between creativity and intelligence in a group of these younger children, although the study was concerned with children of all abilities, and not solely with highly intelligent children.

Wallach and Kogan, who had objected to Getzels and Jackson's proposition that they had produced evidence to show that creativity and intelligence were independent of one another, nevertheless proceeded to investigate the relationship between creativity and intelligence. Their investigation is described in *Modes of Thinking in Young Children* (1965). They obtained scores on three sub-tests of the Wechsler Intelligence Scale for Children, on two tests of scholastic aptitude, and five tests of scholastic achievement, and on ten tests of creativity, from the 81 girls and 70 boys in the fifth grade of a public elementary school in New England, USA. The average age of the pupils was 10 yrs. 7 ms. Some of the creativity tests were verbal, and some were non-verbal. Some of them were clearly derived from the Guilford model of divergent thinking, for example:

> Name all the round things you can think of.
>
> Tell me all the different ways you could use a newspaper/a knife/a shoe.

The responses were scored for total number, and for uniqueness. The writers, however, stress that the test situations were unlike those used by Getzels and Jackson, who had, they claimed, obtained their data in the usual academic evaluative manner of writing under mass conditions and to a time limit. The data obtained in this new study was, on the other hand, obtained in individual situations, with no time limit, and in a friendly and play-like atmosphere; much more conducive, it was claimed, to work of a creative nature. From the data of this study Wallach and Kogan reported that the measures of general intelligence were highly inter-correlated, and also that the measures of creativity were highly inter-correlated, but the correlations *between* the intelligence measures and the creativity measures were very low. They concluded that they had located a dimension of intellectual ability which was independent of general intellectual ability, and was indeed appropriately labelled 'creativity'.

Although many studies have been carried out on creativity, the only reported study of creativity with pupils of comparable age and ability with Terman's sample of children, i.e. between the ages of 8 years and 12 years, and also described as 'intellectually gifted', is that reported by Lovell and Shields (1967).

The general design of the study has already been described (page 21). Measures of intellectual ability were obtained by the Wechsler Verbal, Performance and Full Scale Scores, by a number of Piaget's tests of logical thinking, and by a number of mathematical tests. The tests of divergent thinking (creativity) listed on pages 21-2, were used. They were intended to replicate as far as possible the tests used by Getzels and Jackson (1962), although some modifications were made to suit the younger children. They were given in the pupils' own schools, in a non-competitive atmosphere, and, except in the case of the Hidden Shapes test, without a time limit.

It can be seen from Lovell and Shields (1967) that they were able to compare the scores gained by the children on the creativity tests, not only with the scores gained on the intelligence test, but also with the scores gained on the tests of logical thinking, and the tests of mathematical ability, which were part of the larger investigation. They reported that the comparison indicated the existence of a strong intellective component, common to all the tasks which the children completed, the creativity tests, the conventional test of intelligence, the tasks involving logical thinking, and the tests of mathematical ability. This suggests that creativity tests do not measure intellectual abilities entirely independent of those measured by a conventional test of intelligence, such as the Wechsler Intelligence Scale. However, after due allowance had been made for this large common factor, there was evidence to suggest the existence of creative thinking abilities. They were indicated in the verbal tests, especially in Word Association and in Uses For Things. The ability to make up problems using numerical data was, it should be noted, linked with the ability to work the mathematics tests. It would seem that not only are there differences between individuals in their ability to perform in creativity tasks, but that also individuals may vary in their scores according to the task which is set them.

Lovell and Shields also reported that when they compared the scores obtained on the creativity tests and on the tests of logical thinking with the teachers' ratings for originality, there was a strong positive relationship between scores obtained on tests for logical thinking and teachers' ratings for originality, but there was no relationship between scores on the creativity tests and the originality ratings. Teachers using Terman's Personality Rating Scale, they said, seemed to think of originality in terms of reasoning ability rather than inventiveness or unusual ideas; or possibly the explanation is that 'creativity', as measured by these tests is too specific and at times not easily detected by teachers.

Abilities in divergent thinking tests

The creators of the divergent thinking, creative, or open-ended tests assert that successful performance in them requires the qualities of originality, fluency, flexibility, and elaboration (Guilford, 1962; Torrance, *et al.* 1962).

Several examples of the responses to the creative thinking tests which have been made by pupils between the ages of 12 and 17 years have been published. In *Creativity and*

Intelligence, Getzels and Jackson (1962) have given examples of the responses made by able pupils attending a high school in Chicago. It is clear that some children were good at the tests and some were not good. Hudson (1966) in *Contrary Imaginations* has given examples of the responses made by schoolboys attending grammar and public schools in England. Among the tests which he used were Uses of Objects, and Word Association tests, although for the second test he preferred to use the title 'Meanings of Words'. He also found that some boys were very good indeed at the tests, and some were not so good.

Torrance (1963) has given examples of the responses of young children to a number of tests of divergent thinking. Responses to similar tests, made by gifted children aged 8-11 years in the study reported by Lovell and Shields (1967), are given below. These also show that some pupils appear to answer the questions very well, and others do not. No examples are given here from the Hidden Shapes test. This test seems, on examination, to require convergent thinking rather than divergent thinking, and indeed the scores obtained on the test showed very little correlation with the other tests, the highest correlation coefficient being that of +0·19 with the Word Association test. The examples which follow are from the Fables, Uses for Things, Word Association, and Make-up Problems tests.

Fables

The test material, already outlined in Chapter two, consisted of four incomplete fables. The children were required to compose three different endings to each fable: a moralistic, a humourous, and a sad ending. The ending was required to be a logical outcome of the conditions of the story, and to have the appropriate tone.

This test set a difficult task for children of junior school age. There were, nevertheless, a number of brilliant responses.

FABLE: THE PEACOCK AND THE EAGLE

The peacock, spreading his gorgeous tail, stalked up and down in his most stately manner before an eagle, and ridiculed him for the plainness of his plumage.

'I am robed like a king' said he, 'in gold and purple, and all the colours of the rainbow, while just look at your plain coat.'

'Tut, tut', said the eagle . . .

Children's Responses

A Moralistic Ending

Mary, age 10 years, pursed her lips, took a pencil, and wrote almost immediately:

> 'Tut, tut', said the eagle . . . 'don't judge a book by its cover.'

A Humorous Ending

Stephen, aged 10, wrote:

> 'All kings have a court, where's yours?'

Michael, also aged 10 years, who had revealed a deep interest in and knowledge of classical Greece, wrote:

> 'Tut, tut', said the eagle, ' . . . at the moment I've got on my working clothes.'

Uses for things

The children were asked to write down as many uses as they could think of for five common objects: a brick, a blanket, a pencil, a piece of rope, and a sheet of paper. Marks were awarded for the number of uses, and additional marks were given for uses which were considered to be uncommon (i.e. given by less than one-fifth of the subjects).

A comparison of the responses of two of the children will show the rigidity of thought of one compared with the fluency and flexibility of the other. Fred gave only two uses for a piece of rope. He suggested that it could be 'used to tie things', and 'used to climb'; neither of the uses could be classified as uncommon. William, on the other hand, pointed out eight different uses for the piece of rope: 'Hang someone, hang something, to tie, to make knots on, to climb, to bind, to use as a whip, use as a gun strap'. Some of these uses could be classified as uncommon. The total performance of the two boys on the Uses test can be compared in the following way:

Subject	Age	Wechsler Verbal Score	Wechsler Performance Score	Wechsler Full-Scale Score	Uses Score
Fred	10.10 yrs.	143	127	138	9
William	10.3 yrs.	142	136	143	40

Fred does not have quite such a high IQ score as William, but he is seven months older, and it is surprising to find such a difference in the scores on this test.

Word association

The pupils were required to give as many different meanings as possible to 25 fairly common words such as arm, cap, pink, and tender.

Some children showed a rich and precise grasp of the different meanings of words, and an ability to move freely from one context to another. For example, the following meanings were given by Mary for the word 'Fair'—just, light, feast, moderate; and by Roy for the word 'Punch'—wine, magazine, character, hit. It should be noted that the children were not asked to write the meaning in detail; a sufficient suggestion of the use was all that was required.

Some interesting comparisons of performance can also be made in this test; the scores gained in the Vocabulary Sub-test of the Wechsler Verbal Scale are also included.

1.

Subject	Age	Wechsler Scores			Wechsler Sub-test Vocabulary	Word Association
		V.	*P.*	*F.S.*		
Douglas	8.10	145	146	150	41	27
Janet	9.0	140	146	147	40	51

The two pupils are almost the same age, and have almost equal IQ scores, but Janet has a very much higher score on the test.

2.

Subject	Age	Wechsler IQ Scores			Wechsler Sub-test Vocabulary	Word Association
		V.	*P.*	*F.S.*		
Frank	11.7	145	135	144	43	41
Anne	9.3	148	124	140	40	52

Frank, with a slightly superior IQ score, and an advantage of 2 yrs. 4 ms. in age, clearly does not show the same ability as Anne.

The performance of Richard is particularly interesting:

3.

SUBJECT	AGE	WECHSLER IQ SCORES			WECHSLER SUB-TEST VOCABULARY	WORD ASSOCIATION
		V.	*P.*	*F.S.*		
Richard	10.9	140	125	136	43	27

Although he was one of the oldest children in the group, Richard had a very low score. His inability to supply more than one meaning to each of many common words, for example, 'bolt'—for which he wrote 'fasten', and 'file'—for which he wrote, 'record'—suggests a certain rigidity of thought.

Make-up problems

The test material consisted of three paragraphs, each containing several numerical statements. Each paragraph described a situation whose essential nature was within the experience of the children, such as a school outing, house demolition and building, and a youth club concert. The situations described by Getzels and Jackson were thought to be a little beyond the range of experience of the group, both in general content and in mathematical concepts. In these circumstances different situations were elaborated, and the children were asked to make up as many problems as they could arising from the situations described in each paragraph. There was no time limit.

Example

Mr. Smith is the head teacher of a junior school with 300 pupils. He is taking the 10-year-old pupils for a day's outing by bus. There will be 100 pupils, 60 of whom are girls; 3 other teachers will go with them. The bus fare will be 5s. each. Lunch in a café will cost 2s. 6d. each. There will be packed sandwiches for tea, paid for out of school funds, at a total cost for the pupils' teas of £5; the head and the teachers will pay 3s. each for their packed sandwiches. It will cost 9d. each to go in a museum, 3d. each to go in a ruined castle, and a sail in a boat will cost 6d. each. The children are asked to bring 10s. each, and after all expenses have been met, the money left will be for pocket money. Mr. Smith wanted to be back at school at 5 p.m. because he did not wish to be away for more than 8 hours. However, they were 30 minutes late returning.

Given this information, write down as many problems as you can about the day's outing.

Each of the three situations was successful in stimulating many responses, and there was close agreement in the total number of marks gained in each situation.

Examples of the problems constructed by the children are:

1. How many boys are going on the trip?
2. What fraction of the school children are going on the outing?
3. How much will be paid altogether for bus fare?
4. How much will it cost to provide one pupil with a packed tea?
5. How much cheaper per person is it to go in a ruined castle than a museum?
6. At what time did the children set off?
7. What is the cost of the boys' bus fares and lunch?

As in the case of the other tests some interesting comparisons of scores can be made.

1.

SUBJECT	AGE	WECHSLER SCORES			MAKE-UP PROBLEMS
		Verbal	*Performance*	*Full-Scale*	
David	9.9 yrs.	143	122	136	195
William	10.3 yrs.	142	136	143	78

David, who is near the middle of the age group, and has one of the lower IQ scores, obtained a very high number of marks on this test. William, who did so well in the Uses test, is six months older, and has a better IQ score, obtained the second lowest total of marks.

2.

SUBJECT	AGE	WECHSLER SCORES			MAKE-UP PROBLEMS
		Verbal	*Performance*	*Full-Scale*	
Paul	10.8 yrs.	147	139	147	86
Stanley	8.7 yrs.	142	139	144	136

The scores of these two boys contrast sharply. Paul, one of the oldest of the group, with high IQ scores (and also high scores on the mathematical tests) has a low total of marks. Stanley, who is two years younger, and has a slightly lower IQ score, leads him on this test by as many as 50 points.

References

BURT, C. (1949). 'The structure of the mind', *Brit. J. Educ. Psychol.*, 19, pp. 196-99.

BURT, C. (1962a). 'General introduction: the gifted child'. In: BEREDAY, G. Z. F. and LAUWERYS, J. A. eds. *The Year Book of Education 1962.* London: Evans.

BURT, C. (1962b). 'Critical notice: creativity and intelligence by J. W. GETZELS and P. W. JACKSON', *Brit. J. Educ. Psychol.*, 32, pp. 292-98.

CROPLEY, A. J. (1966). 'Creativity and intelligence', *Brit. J. Educ. Psychol.*, 36, pp. 259-66.

GALTON, F. (1869). *Hereditary Genius.* London: Collins.

GETZELS, J. W. and JACKSON, P. W. (1962). *Creativity and Intelligence.* London and New York: Wiley.

HARRIS, C. W. and LIBA, M. R. (1965). 'Component, image and factor analysis and tests of intellect and motor performance', *Co-operative Research Project*, No. 3-192-64. University of Wisconsin.

HUDSON, L. (1966). *Contrary Imaginations.* New York: Schocken.

KOESTLER, A. (1964). *The Act of Creation.* London: Hutchinson.

LOVELL, K. and SHIELDS, J. B. (1967). 'Some aspects of a study of the gifted child', *Brit. J. Educ. Psychol.*, 37, pp. 201-9.

MARSH, R. W. (1964). 'Research note: a statistical re-analysis of Getzels and Jackson's data', *Brit. J. Educ. Psychol.*, 34, pp. 91-3.

SULTAN, E. E. (1962). 'A factorial study in the domain of creative thinking', *Brit. J. Educ. Psychol.*, 32, pp. 78-82.

TORRANCE, E. P. (1962). 'Measurement and development of the creative thinking abilities'. In: BEREDAY, G. Z. F. and LAUWERYS, J. A. eds. *The Year Book of Education 1962.* London: Evans; Chapter 6, pp. 125–42.

VERNON, P. E. (1964). 'Creativity and intelligence', *Educ. Res.*, Vol. 3, pp. 163-9.

WALLACH, M. A. and KOGAN, N. (1965). *Modes of Thinking in Young Children.* New York: Holt, Rinehart & Winston.

YAMOMOTO, K. (1965). 'Effects of restriction of range and test unreliability on correlation between measures of intelligence and creative thinking', *Brit. J. Educ. Psychol.*, 35, pp. 300-5.

Chapter Four

Logical Thinking

THE studies of gifted children reported in chapters two and three were of children described as 'gifted' because of their outstandingly high intellectual ability. In the majority of the investigations, intellectual ability was assessed by the use of an individual standardized test of intelligence. The Stanford-Binet Scale was used in Terman's Californian investigation, the Terman-Merrill Revised Version of the Stanford-Binet Scale was used by Parkyn in New Zealand, and the Wechsler Intelligence Scale for Children was employed in the north of England study reported by Lovell and Shields (op. cit. 1967). In the remaining studies, intellectual ability was assessed by the use of a number of tests of divergent thinking, tests which originated in the convergency-divergency sector of Guilford's model of the structure of the intellect. The children identified in this way have been described subsequently as 'creatively gifted', especially by Getzels and Jackson in their investigation of the relationship between creativity and intelligence.

There is, however, another important model of both the nature and the mode of development of intelligence. This is the model constructed by Professor Jean Piaget, frequently acknowledged as a most stimulating explanation of intellectual development. This view is clearly taken by Berlyne (1957) and by Flavell (1963). Berlyne wrote: '. . . Piaget is, without doubt, one of the most outstanding figures of contemporary psychology, and his contributions will eventually have to be reckoned with much more than they are, both in the management of children and in many areas which may not seem directly connected with child psychology'. Flavell wrote: 'Piaget's system is by far the richest repository of theory and data on intellectual psychology that is or ever has been available in the field of child psychology'. There is, in fact, a widespread interest in Piaget's model of intellectual development.

There is also a growing recognition of the importance of logical thought, well-expressed by Lovell (1961b): 'Logical thought is the most powerful tool that man has for coming to grips with the matter-energy system'. It is therefore rather surprising to find an absence of investigations of the abilities and characteristics of children who might be regarded as gifted, or outstandingly able, in logical thinking. Certainly there are no reported studies of the growth of logical thinking in children who were initially identified as gifted. However, the gifted children in the study reported by Lovell and Shields were examined and assessed in a number of Piaget's experimental situations. The tests used were:

1. Equilibrium in the Balance (Inhelder and Piaget, 1958)
2. Combinations of Colourless Liquids (Inhelder and Piaget, 1958)
3. The Oscillation of a Pendulum (Inhelder and Piaget, 1958)
4. The Concept of Volume (Lovell and Ogilvie, 1961).

The pupils were also asked to complete a number of tasks requiring for their correct solution an understanding of the concept of proportion.

From the results of the experiments it is possible to make some statements about the logical thinking abilities of the group of gifted children. But before the experimental situations are described and the results given, it would perhaps be helpful to give an account of some aspects of Piaget's model of intellectual development.

Piaget (1950) has described his view of the nature and growth of intelligence in *The Psychology of Intelligence*. He is primarily interested in those aspects of intelligence which are concerned with 'knowing'. He recognizes the presence and the importance of the 'affective functions', or emotions, in providing the goals of human behaviour and supplying the energy to pursue them, but his own interest lies predominantly in the cognitive processes which make possible the attainment of the ends to which the energy is directed. He sees 'knowing' as occurring through the growth of mental structures. These structures are subject to a hierarchial organization, in that one structure at a lower level of development is not able to perform the mental acts which may be carried out by another structure which is of more advanced development. Intelligence, therefore, may be defined as 'only a generic term to indicate the superior forms of organization or equilibrium of cognitive structurings' (Piaget, op. cit.).

There are, in Piaget's view, a number of principal periods or stages in the development of intelligence (Piaget, op. cit. 1950).

Sensori-Motor Intelligence (Birth to 1½/2 yrs.)
Pre-Conceptual Thought (2-4 yrs.) } Pre-Operational
Intuitive Thought (4-7 yrs.) } Thought
Concrete Operations (7-11 yrs.)
Formal Operations (11/12 yrs. to adolescence)

In considering the logical thinking abilities of the gifted child of junior school age, the first two stages of sensori-motor intelligence and pre-conceptual thought are omitted.

The stage of intuitive thought

During this period there are certainly ways in which the child shows intellectual development. He increases his vocabulary considerably, and because his vocabulary is larger he can share much more in the normal activities of family and school life. He can obey verbal instructions, and is therefore not restricted to being shown how to act. He can give an account, in simple language, of his own experiences, tell of things he has seen and heard, and of how he feels. However, in spite of these developments, the child's thinking is still strongly affected by what he perceives. There are still occasions when he shows that he cannot deal with more than one aspect of a problem at a time; this leads him to make many illogical conclusions of the kind which can be illustrated in the following manner.

In the early days of this stage he may carry out the physical actions to establish correspondence between two numerically equal sets of objects by, for example, putting glasses by the side of bottles, or eggs by the side of egg cups. But it can be clearly seen that although the child may initially set up correspondence between the objects, he cannot maintain it if the objects are distributed in the spatial field in such a manner that the actual physical one-to-one relationship is destroyed, as when one group of objects is bunched closer together and occupies less space, or one group is spread out and occupies more space. This phenomenon, in which thought is dominated by perception and shows a certain illogicality, may be seen not only in the case of discontinuous quantities, as described above, but in the case of continuous quantities as when the shape of a lump of plasticene is changed, or when a quantity of liquid is poured into a container of different shape. Here again, the child shows that he concentrates on one aspect of the situation; when the object which was short and fat becomes longer but thinner, he will say that there is more of the object because he is unable to co-ordinate the dimensions.

The stage of concrete operations

The child's thinking from 7-11 years reveals that when it is concerned with the real world of concrete objects and events it conforms to the requirements of logical thinking. The child is now able to look in on and monitor his own thinking and see the part which he is playing in the ordering of his experiences. He now rejects completely the idea that liquid increases in amount when poured from one vessel to another which is taller and thinner; indeed during this period the child's thinking becomes sufficiently systematic to give him some consistent understanding of the concrete world. With these abilities, he is able to build up some of the basic concepts which help him to make sense of the real world, such as concepts of number, of time, and of area.

The development of these concepts is a slow and gradual process; Inhelder (1964) writes: 'Thus, during the course of this second period of development, we can follow the genesis of thought processes which—at about seven years of age—issues in the elementary logico-mathematical thought structures. Nevertheless, it still requires years before these structures are brought to bear on all possible concrete contents. It can be shown, for example, that the principle of invariance (constancy, conservation) is applied earlier to the quantity of matter than to weight, and still later to volume'.

The stage of formal operations

At this stage, from 11 years into adolescence, logical thinking advances from the realm of concrete situations to that of hypothetical situations. The pupil can, when presented with certain data, set up a hypothesis and work out what would happen if the hypothesis were true. An example of this can be seen in the experiment dealing with the oscillation of a pendulum (op. cit. 1958). The pupil is given the necessary apparatus of string and weights and asked to find which of the four factors—the weight of the bob, the length of the string, the strength of the push, or the height of the drop—controls the rate at which the bob swings from side to side as in a pendulum. The pupil can propose, for example, that it is the weight of the bob which controls the rate of oscillation, and he can organize a means of testing the proposition. The pupil is only able to solve the problem if he is able to isolate each of the variables, and test each in turn, while holding all other factors constant so that the effectiveness or ineffectiveness of each may be determined.

It can be understood that propositional reasoning of this degree of complexity requires the person to possess a combinatorial system which will allow him to handle the many variables present in the problem. This ability to handle second order operations allows the pupil to develop the schema of proportion. An example of this can be seen in mathematics. In understanding such a statement as 3 is to 8 as 9 is to 24, the pupil has to see the relationship between 3 and 8, and the relationship between 9 and 24, and then he has to make a comparison between the relationships. Thinking at this degree of abstraction is, in Piaget's view, typical of the stage of formal thought, which permits the pupil to theorize about action in many areas.

Research studies

Piaget's view of the ages during which the development of both concrete and formal operational thinking takes place is given on page 123 of *The Psychology of Intelligence* (1950), as follows:

> 'From 7-8 years to 11-12 years "concrete operations" are organized. . .'

and

> 'Finally, from 11-12 years and during adolescence, formal thought is perfected . . .'

In support of these statements Piaget has provided numerous accounts of individual children's responses to various experimental situations. These are published in many of his books, and especially in *The Growth of Logical Thought* (1958), which was written in collaboration with Professor Barbel Inhelder. Piaget does not say how many of the children were classified at each of the stages of logical thought; neither does he give any other indication of the mental ability of the children. Since the publication of *The Growth of Logical Thought*, however, there have been a number of investigations designed to produce information of this kind. Lodwick (1958) made a study of a group of children's thinking about some historical passages which were read to them. Case and Collinson (1962) made a similar study of pupils aged 7 to 17 years, using texts of history, geography, and literature. Goldman (1962) reported a study of children's thinking in answer to questions about a number of Bible stories. All these studies found that mental age was a somewhat better guide to a child's logical thinking ability than chronological age.

Lovell (1961a), has carried out a substantial replication of ten of the experiments described by Inhelder and Piaget in *The Growth of Logical Thought*. In this investigation, 200 subjects, varying in age from 8-32 years, were examined individually in four experiments. Among the 200 subjects were 34 able and bright junior school pupils, and 14 average and bright preparatory school pupils. From this study Lovell reported that 'it is only rarely that average to bright junior school children reach the stage of formal operations'.

The question whether the teacher in the junior school with pupils between the ages of 8-12 years may expect the gifted child to think consistently, or even occasionally, at the formal operational level is one of considerable importance, and has been investigated in the recent study of the gifted child by Lovell and Shields (1967).

As reported on page 63, each of the fifty children was examined individually on four tests: The Concept of Volume (Lovell and Ogilvie, 1961); Equilibrium in the Balance, Combinations of Colourless Chemical Bodies, and The Oscillation of a Pendulum. Each child, after being made familiar with the apparatus, was asked to solve problems which required the carrying out of certain actions. He was then asked to explain his actions and supplementary questions were used to make clear the reasons for his actions. The child's actions were noted and his replies recorded.

Each child was also asked a number of questions requiring for their correct solution an understanding of the schema of proportion.

The concept of volume

Piaget has given his view that an understanding of volume begins to arise at about the age of 6-7 years, and that it appears to be established at about the age of 12-13 years. He describes in more detail the gradual progression from an understanding of, for example, the space within a box, which is 'interior volume', to an understanding of the space which is taken up by something, which is 'occupied volume', and subsequently to an understanding that the actual occupying of space implies the displacement of something else, which is an understanding of 'displacement volume'.

Wallace (1965), has summarized investigations upon the topic made by Lunzer (1960), Lovell and Ogilvie (1961), Elkind (1961), and Beard (1962). The most interesting study of the seven- to twelve-year-old child is described by Lovell and Ogilvie (1961), who reported: 'It is clear that an understanding of physical volume in any generalized sense does not develop until late in the life of the junior school child, and even then there are many gaps in his knowledge' (op. cit., 1961).

The volume test procedures used by Lovell and Ogilvie were used by the writer in the course of the study of the fifty gifted children. The apparatus used was a gallon can, a pint can, a quantity of water, and twenty-five aluminium cubes.

From the answers which the children gave to a number of questions we may say that they understood both 'interior volume' and 'occupied volume', and almost all of them had some understanding of 'displacement volume', because they said that if a number of aluminium cubes (twelve arranged to form a block $2 \times 3 \times 2$) were placed in a gallon can which was full of water, some water would spill over the side. But not all the children who understood displacement in the instance described maintained the understanding when the size of the object to be immersed, or the size of the liquid containers, was changed. Only thirty-six of the children understood that the amounts of water displaced by a single cube when immersed in a full pint can and in a full gallon can were the same; while only twenty-six of them grasped that the amounts of water displaced by two cubes of the same size and shape, but different weights were equal.

It was clear, therefore, that in some cases the children's thinking was not stable; it was affected by such factors as the size of the can and the weight of the cubes. For example, one child who had asserted that the amount of water displaced by a block of 12 cubes would always be the same—i.e. the actual physical arrangement, in a block, or distributed quite separately, did not matter because the cubes would always take up the same room—nevertheless stated that one cube would displace more water from a pint can full of water than from a gallon can full of water. A number of children who had understood that the amount of water displaced by a single cube did not vary according to the size of the container, were nevertheless of the opinion that the amount of water displaced would vary according to the weight of the cube, i.e. the heavier the cube the greater the amount of water displaced. Doris, who was typical of the children who gave an incorrect reply to the question involving weight, said:

'Definitely there would be more spilt over with the lead (as opposed to aluminium) because it's heavier'.

If we examine the responses made by the gifted children, and compare them with the replies given in the unselected sample of 2nd-, 3rd- and 4th-year junior school children studied by Lovell and Ogilvie (1961), the developmental position of the gifted children is made clearer.

TABLE 4: TABLE SHOWING NUMBERS AND PERCENTAGES OF CHILDREN SUCCESSFUL IN ALL TESTS: (a) GIFTED CHILDREN
(b) UNSELECTED CHILDREN

AGE IN YRS. AND MS.	NUMBER OF CHILDREN		NUMBER OF CHILDREN SUCCESSFUL		PERCENTAGE OF CHILDREN SUCCESSFUL	
	Gifted	*Unselected*	*Gifted*	*Unselected*	*Gifted*	*Unselected*
8.5 - 9.5	12	40	5	5	42	12
9.6 - 10.5	21	45	10	5	46	11
10.6 - 11.7	17	55	9	21	53	38
8.5 - 11.7	50	140	24	31	48	22

The results indicate that nearly half (47 per cent) of the gifted children did not show a complete understanding of volume, as measured by these tests, even during the fourth year of junior school life. But the figures also suggest that the thinking of outstandingly bright junior children of eight and nine years of age is very much more flexible than that of ordinary children, for in the age group $8\frac{1}{2}$-$9\frac{1}{2}$ years, 42 per cent of the gifted were successful as compared with only $12\frac{1}{2}$ per cent of the unselected children, and the percentages in the $9\frac{1}{2}$-$10\frac{1}{2}$ years group were 46 and 11 per cent respectively. The proportion of the younger gifted pupils who answered all the questions successfully (42 per cent) is not greatly different from the proportion of older pupils (53 per cent) passing all the tests; this suggests that the thinking of the gifted child is very flexible from quite early days in the junior school.

Timothy, aged eight years, showed that he had a very fine understanding of the concept of volume. His answers to a number of questions are reproduced on the following pages.

A. Interior Volume

1. Here we have two blocks of bricks (2/2/3) and (2/3/2).

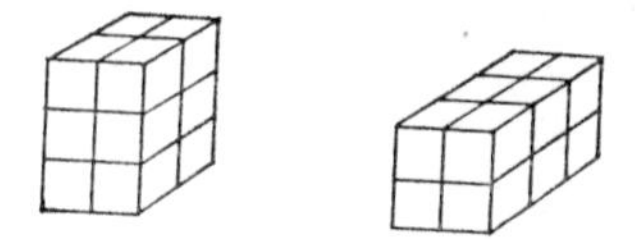

Examiner: If we made two boxes, one for each block of bricks, so that there was just enough room in each box to hold the bricks, would there be as much room in one box as in the other?

Timothy: There would be the same.

Examiner: How do you know?

Timothy: Although they look different, they really are the same; the same number.

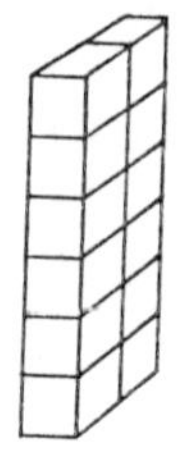

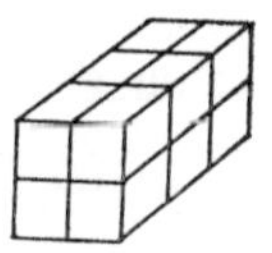

Examiner: If we make another box with just enough room in it to hold this block of bricks (1/2/6), would that box have the same amount of room in it as this box (2/3/2)?

Timothy: Yes.

Examiner: How do you know?

Timothy: Although this one is taller (pointing to the 1/2/6), this one (2/3/2) is wider.

B. Occupied Volume

'Before we fill this can (1 gallon) with water we are going to put some bricks in like this.' (The block 2/3/2 is placed in the gallon can.)

1.

'If we now fill this can to the top, do we still get the same amount of water in as before, or do the bricks make a difference?'

'They make a difference.'

'Why do you say that?'

'Because if it is full, the bricks take up room, thus causing the water to overflow.'

The block 2/3/2 was removed from the can.

2.

'Suppose we put this block (1/2/6) into the 1 gallon can. Are we able to get as much water into the can now as we could with this block (2/3/2) in the can?'

'Just as much water.'

'Why do you say that?'

'Because it (1/2/6) is tall and narrow and this (2/3/2) is short and wide.'

'Does it matter how the blocks are arranged?'

'No.'

'Why do you say that?'

'Because there is the same number of blocks if you put it in any way.'

C. Displacement Volume

The block (1/2/6) was removed from the can. The water was left in the pint can.

'Let's pretend that the gallon can is full of water right to the top just like the pint can, and that I place this block of bricks (2/3/2) very carefully into the gallon can so that there is no splash.'

1.

'Is it possible to put the bricks (2/3/2) into the pint can very carefully without spilling any water?'

'No.'

'Why do you say that?'

'Because the bricks take up room.'

2.

'What happens if you place these bricks (1/2/6) in the pint can instead of these (2/3/2)?'

'Spill over.'

'What do you know about the amounts of water spilt over?'

'Both the same.'

'Why do you say that?'

'Because although it looks different, it isn't.'

One separate block was shown to the child.

3.

'If just one block was lowered into the full pint can, would any water spill over?'

'Yes.'

'If just one block was lowered into the full gallon can, would any water spill over?'

'Yes.'

'Would the amounts spilt be the same?'

'Yes.'

'Why do you say that?'

'Because although the sides of the cans are different (he ran his fingers round the edge of the gallon can), the size of the block is the same.'

4.

'What can you tell me about the amounts of water spilt over if I put just one of these blocks, which is made of aluminium, in a full pint can, and if I put just one block of exactly the same size and shape, but made of lead and therefore much heavier, in another full pint can?'

'The water spilt over would be the same, because although lead is heavier, it is the same size, thus taking up the same room.'

In summary, we may say that some gifted children of eight and nine years of age show an extraordinary grasp of the concept of volume. They have learnt to eliminate irrelevant factors so that they understand 'interior', 'occupied' and 'displacement' volume. There are, however, a good number of junior school children of the highest intellectual ability, as measured by IQ, who have gaps in their understanding of physical volume.

The three tests:

Equilibrium in the balance; combination of colourless liquids; the oscillation of a pendulum.

In *The Growth of Logical Thinking* (B. Inhelder and J. Piaget, 1958), these three tests are described and examples of the responses made to them by a number of children are given. The testing procedure used by Inhelder and Piaget was very much a clinical one in that the examiner presented the apparatus and the problem to the children, and then permitted them to experiment rather freely. At the same time he encouraged them to talk and give reasons for their actions wherever possible. In the experiments reported here (Lovell and Shields, 1967), which sought to combine the clinical approach with a measure of standardization, the procedure adopted by Lovell (1966) of making sure that a small number of common questions were put to each child, was followed. Professor Inhelder has written in *The Growth of Basic Mathematical and Scientific Concepts* (Lovell, 1961b) of the general success of this method.

In the balance experiment the pupil was presented with a balance and supporting framework made of meccano strips. The arm contained 24 holes, numbered from the centre, on either side of the fulcrum. He was shown five weights of 1, 2, 5, 10 and 20 grammes respectively, and was then required to solve a number of problems, two of which are described.

First, he was asked to place the 5 gms. weight in hole 18 on one side of the balance arm, and the 10 gms. weight in hole 10 on the other side of the arm, so that the arm took up the position shown in the diagram below. He was then asked to make the balance arm straight, and to explain his actions.

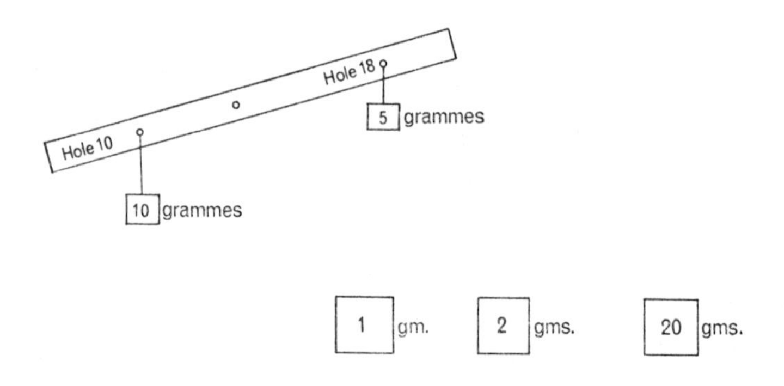

In another problem, he was asked to place the 20 gms. weight at hole 10 and the 1 gm. weight at hole 20 on the same side. Then, he was asked to place the 10 gms. weight and the 2 gms. weight in position, so as to make the arm straight. The situation can be seen in the diagram on the next page.

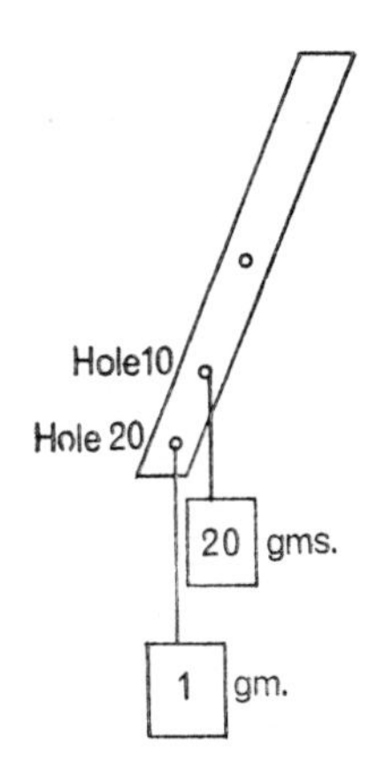

In the chemicals experiment, the pupil was shown five bottles, each containing a colourless and odourless liquid. The bottles were marked 1, 2, 3, 4 and g, respectively.

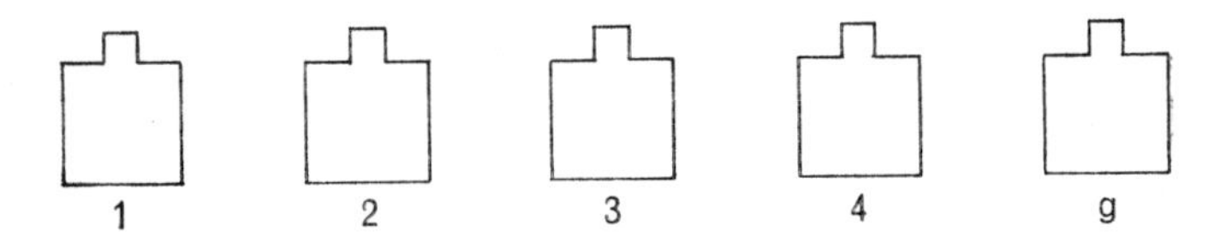

The pupil was also shown two beakers, each containing a small amount of liquid. Unknown to him, one beaker contained liquid from bottles 1 and 3, and the other beaker contained liquid from bottle number 2. The child was asked to observe while a few drops from the bottle marked 'g' were poured into each of the beakers.

The combination 1+3+g produced a yellow colour, while the liquid in the second beaker was unchanged. The pupil was then asked to reproduce the yellow colour, using any or all of the bottles as he wished (bottle number 4 had a neutralizing effect; bottle number 2 contained water).

In the pendulum experiment, he was supplied with a projecting metal arm, a piece of string, and four weights of 20, 50, 100, and 200 gms. respectively. He was set the task of assessing which factor was responsible for the varying rate of oscillation of the string acting as a pendulum: the weight, the length of string, the height of the drop, or the impetus given to the weight.

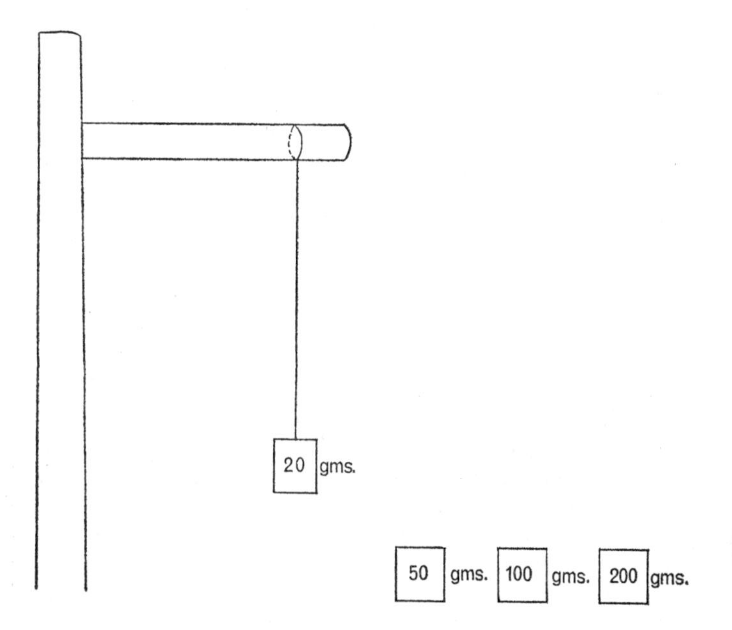

The responses to the balance, chemicals and pendulum experiments were assessed at Piaget's main and sub-stages, but additional intermediate stages were also used, making eleven levels of performance in all, as follows, 1A, 1AB, 1B, 1B/2A—pre-operational; 2A, 2AB, 2B, 2B/3A—concrete operations; 3A, 3AB, 3B—formal operations.

TABLE SHOWING THE DISTRIBUTION OF THE STAGES REACHED

EXPERIMENT	1B/2A	2A	2AB	2B	2B/3A	3A	3AB	3B
Balance	2	3	12	21	7	5	0	0
Chemicals	0	12	16	15	4	1	1	1
Pendulum	1	7	13	13	9	5	2	0
TOTAL	3	22	41	49	20	11	3	1
Percentage distribution of responses	Pre-operational 2	Concrete Operations 88				Formal Operations 10		

The table shows that with few exceptions, the eight to eleven-year-old children were assessed at the stage of concrete operations. Many of the children were well-advanced in concrete operations, for in 56 per cent of the experimental situations the responses were classified at stage 2B or higher.

In the balance experiment 66 per cent of the children revealed that they could act on the hypothesis that the same object 'will weigh more' at a greater distance from the axis, and 'less' when it is brought closer to it, and were accordingly classified at the 2B stage of concrete operations, or higher. They were also frequently able to give a good explanation of their actions:

Anne said: 'The nearer it gets to the centre, it weighs less, sort of thing; if it gets right to the end it weighs a lot more.'

Timothy said: 'If it's a long way from the centre it seems to give that . . . er . . . it gives more weight; if it's a short way, as it's nearer, it doesn't give so much weight.'

Charles said: 'A weight, when it is nearer to the centre, affects the balance by making it as though the weight was lighter. When the weight is further away, it is as if the weight is heavier, so that a heavy weight can be balanced by a light weight that is further away from the centre than it.'

In the chemicals experiment, 44 per cent of the children were thinking at an advanced level of concrete operations. They showed that they could combine two factors with 'g', although not necessarily systematically. Douglas for example, responded in the following manner:

'4+g, No; 4+g+2, No; 4+g+2+3, No; 4+g+2+3+1, No. I'll have to try again. I'll try 2+3+g, No. I'll add a bit of 1; 2+3+g+1.' (The liquid in the beaker turned yellow.) 'That's it.'

Examiner: Do you need all those (i.e. liquids)?

Douglas: Maybe, maybe not. I'll try 2+1+g; No. I think that you do . . . unless it's just 1+3+g. (Tried them, and the liquid in the beaker turned yellow.) Yes, that's it.

Examiner: Suppose that you hadn't got the colour. What would you do?

Douglas: 3+2+g, (tried them) No. (He then tried 3+g, 1+g, 2+g.) No good. I think I've tried everything now . . . I could try 4+1+g. (Tried them) No . . . I've tried everything now . . . except 4+3+g (tried them) No. I wish there was something else I could do.

The example above reveals a performance in advance of John, whose operations were limited. He put all the liquids in one beaker with 'g' (viz. 4+2+g+3+1).

Moreover his subsequent actions were confined to either the addition of liquid, or to the alteration of the order, as follows:

John: A bit more g, a bit more 3. Have you got to do it in a certain order? (He then combined 1 and 3 and g.) That's it, yellow.

Examiner: If it had not turned yellow, what would you have done?

John: Put a bit more of 1 and 3 and g. Tried them in every order I could think of.

Examiner: Tell me.

John: 1+2+3+4+g. g+4+3+2+1, that is the other way round.

In the pendulum experiment 58 per cent of the children were thinking at an advanced level of concrete operations. They showed that they could take the variables one at a time, and make a judgement upon the observations, frequently seeing the relationship between the length of the string and the rate of the oscillations, but they also frequently changed more than one variable at a time, as may be seen in the following example.

Tom suspended the 200 gms. weight and released it from a low dropping point. He watched and then said: 'I'll change the string'. He shortened the string and released the same weight from the same point of height. He noticed that the weight swung from side to side at a faster rate. 'That's it. The shorter the string, the faster the pendulum swings.' After a pause he said: 'I'll try a longer string'. Whereupon he lengthened the string, and used the same weight, but this time he failed to keep the variables constant, because he changed the position of release of the weight from a low point to a high one. Later in the experiment, when considering the effect of weight upon the oscillations, he again changed two variables. First he used a 200 gms.

weight, a long string and a low dropping point. Then he changed the weight to 25 gms., but he also shortened the string. His conclusion that 'the lighter the weight the faster it goes', was erroneous and without justification.

These procedures contrast quite sharply with the quality of thought typical of the formal stage. The subject at the latter stage of thinking is able to isolate all the variables, and systematically work through all possible combinations, excluding those variables which are shown to be irrelevant. Further he would not seem to be regulating his behaviour in a 'trial and error' manner, but would tend to show rather that from the outset he had a comprehensive grasp of the situation.

In only ten per cent of the experiments were the children's responses rated at the formal operational level, and over 70 per cent of these were not at an advanced level of formal operations. Two examples of advanced operational thinking among these junior school pupils are given:

Charles, aged nine, carried out the experiment with the colourless chemical bodies in the following manner.

Examiner: Now, please make the yellow colour for me.

The boy took a small beaker, and poured in a few drops from each bottle.

Charles: 4+g, No; 4+g+2, No; 4+g+2+1, No; 4+g+2+1+3, No. So, it must be just one, or two or three of these, (pointing to the bottles numbered 1, 2, 3 and 4) not all of them. (He took another beaker.) 1+g, No; 1+g+3. (The yellow colour appeared) That's it.

Examiner: If you had not obtained the colour, what would you have done?

Charles: I would have added 2, and then I would have started again with g+1+3+4. (He tried these, and noting the neutralizing effect of 4, remarked) Mm, 4 takes away the colour.

Examiner: How could you be sure which bottles do it?

Charles: Well, I would use 1+g, 2+g, 3+g, 4+g, separately of course. If that didn't work, I would put g+1+2, and then . . . (here he enumerated the six combinations of two variables, each time with g) And that is all the possible ways of doing it with three liquids. Then, g+1+2+3; g+2+3+4; g+1+3+4; g+1+2+4; . . . I think that is all . . . The only other way is to combine them all.

Examiner: What about number 4?

Charles: That takes the yellow colour away.

Anthony, aged nine, responded to one of the tasks in the balance experiment in the following manner:

Examiner: Place the 20 gms. weight at hole 10, and the 1 gm. weight at hole 20 on the one side. Now, will you place the 10 gms. weight and the 2 gms. weight on the other side so as to make the arm straight.

The boy almost immediately placed the 10 gms. weight at hole 20, and the 2 gms. weight at hole 10, and said: 'The 10 gms. weight weighs half as much as the 20, so, if the 20 is near the middle at number 10, you make it equal by putting the 10 at number 20, so that it will pull down more to make it equal; and it's the same thing with the 2 and the 1'.

The level of the children's performances varied in each experiment, although in some instances the gradings were similar. For example, one child was graded at Stage 2A/B in all three experiments, another at Stage 2B, and another at Stage 3A. There was, in fact, a general similarity between the scores obtained on each of the tests; the correlation coefficients between the tests were positive but not high, the highest being that between the chemicals and the pendulum experiments, where r equalled 0·50. It is clear, however, that the pupils did show some variation in their performance according to the field of operation, for one child was graded at Stage 2A, 2A/B, and Stage 2B/3A in the three experiments.

The schema of proportion

Piaget takes the view that the schema of proportion is not available until the age of twelve when the development of formal operations begins. Support for this view has been given by Lovell (1961a, 1966), Lunzer (1965), Lunzer and Pumfrey (1966), and Lovell and Butterworth (1966). It is interesting to look at the performance of the group of 50 gifted children in certain types of numerical series and analogies which require for their solution the schema of proportion. It will be remembered that these children were not only outstanding in their IQ scores, but also obtained very high scores on Vernon's Graded Arithmetic-Mathematics Test. In addition, they obtained high scores on a number of tests compiled by the National Foundation for Educational Research (Lovell and Shields, 1967). For example, in the Mathematical Insight Test (14+), which was completed by the twenty-five oldest children, the mean score for the group was 47, and the conversion table indicated that this would have given a quotient of 107 to a subject aged 15 yrs. 1 m. So we can say that the performance of the gifted group with a mean age for the twenty-five oldest subjects of 10 yrs. 6 ms. more than matched that of the 'average' pupil who was 4 yrs. 7 ms. older. One child, Brian, aged 10 yrs. 5 ms., achieved a score of 71, which would have gained a quotient as high as 127 for a pupil who was 4 yrs. 8 ms. older. It is important to note that in spite of these high scores in tests of intellectual ability, mathematical attainment, and mathematical ability, the children experienced the greatest difficulty with some of the series and analogies which they were asked to complete. Whereas forty-eight children could continue the series 48, 24, 12, 6 . . ., only eleven could continue the series 16, 24, 36,

54 . . ., and only five could answer the questions: '3 is to 7 as 9 is to . . .', and '2 is to . . . is to 8 as 3 is to 9 is to . . .' It may be noted that of the five pupils who successfully answered the question: '3 is to 7 as 9 is to . . .', two were at the stage of formal thought in the balance experiment and one was at the borderline stage of 2B/3A. This finding is also another illustration of the point that formal thinking is not available to the child in all situations at first.

Levels of ability

In the preceding pages some details have been given o the logical thinking abilities of a group of gifted children aged 8-11 years tested in a number of experimental situations.

It was rarc to find an occasion when the abilities of the child functioned at Piaget's pre-operational level. The children were typically well-established in the stage of concrete operational thinking, but it was only occasionally that they showed themselves capable of formal thought. This was reflected in their lack of complete understanding of the concept of volume, of a combinatorial system which could deal with a number of variables, or of ability to deal with the schema of proportion. Further, for classification at the formal operational level, Piaget requires a certain degree of spontaneity of action in the experimental situations. The children in this study, although they were of the highest intellectual ability as measured by IQ, did not on the whole meet these criteria.

In these conclusions there is support for Piaget's view that: 'From 7-8 years to 11-12 years "concrete operations" are organized . . .' And: 'Finally, from 11-12 years and during adolescence formal thought is perfected'.

It might be thought therefore, that the gifted child of 9, 10 or 11 years of age is not similarly gifted in logical thinking, since his thinking is typically at the concrete operational level. There are, however, a number of studies, for example Hughes (1965), Lovell (1961a), Goldman

(1962) and Hallam (1967), which suggest that the logical thinking of the average child three, four or five years older than the gifted child of junior school age is also typically at the concrete operational level, which suggests that notwithstanding the considerable difference in age, the pupils are at the same level of ability in logical thinking.

Hughes (1965) reported a four-year longitudinal study of the growth of logical thinking in a group of 40 secondary-modern school children; the mean IQ score of the group was 99. The children were asked to carry out four of the experiments described by Inhelder and Piaget (1958), including the balance, chemicals, and pendulum experiments. Their responses were classified at the pre-operational, concrete operational and formal operational levels. There is a close similarity between the performance of the gifted junior-school pupils, and the performance of the secondary-modern school pupils at the age of 14+.

TABLE SHOWING THE PERCENTAGE OF RESPONSES CLASSIFIED AT THE PRE-OPERATIONAL, CONCRETE AND FORMAL OPERATIONAL LEVELS

	Pre-Operational	Concrete Operational	Formal Operational
8-11 yrs. gifted mean IQ 144	2	88	10
14-15 yrs. mean IQ 99	6	87	7

These figures indicate that the performance of the gifted junior-school child in logical thinking is equal to the performance of the average pupil who is three, four or five years older. There was, of course, an indication of this in Lovell's investigation reported in 1961. In this investigation, 200 subjects, varying in age from children of eight years to adults and covering a wide range of ability, were examined in ten of the experimental situations described by Inhelder and Piaget, and again the balance, chemicals and pendulum experiments were used. It was clearly shown that the less able secondary-modern school pupils of fifteen years of age were at a low level of logical thought.

In his study of children's religious thinking (1961), Goldman found that formal thought did not appear until the subjects had reached a mental age of 13.5 to 14.2 yrs. Hallam (1967) has reported an investigation of children's logical thinking when answering questions on a number of historical passages. There were 100 pupils drawn from each of the first five years in a large, country secondary school. The answers to the questions were graded at the pre-operational, concrete and formal operational levels. An extract from Table VII (*op. cit.* 1967, p. 190) is given below.

AVERAGE NUMBER OF PRE-OPERATIONAL, CONCRETE AND FORMAL THOUGHT ANSWERS PER CHILD IN MENTAL AGE GROUPS (OTIS D) FOR 100 SUBJECTS

For the three stories

Mental Age	Pre-operational	Concrete	Formal	Number in Group
14+ to 17+	0·18	2·02	0·80	61
10+ to 13+	1·18	1·80	0·03	39

For the five questions

Mental Age	Pre-operational	Concrete	Formal	Number in Group
14+ to 17+	1·33	3·18	0·49	61
10+ to 13+	3·26	1·74	0·00	39

It can be seen that in both groups of pupils, which included children of high mental age, the vast majority of the answers were graded below the level of formal thought. The majority of the answers of the pupils with mental ages between 14+ and 17+ years were placed at the concrete operational level. Hallam concluded from his investigation that a mental age of at least 16 years was required for formal thinking in history.

In addition to these reports of the general existence of concrete operational thought, even in later adolescence, attention may be given to the statistical treatment of the scores made by the fifty children drawn from schools in two cities in the north of England (op. cit., 1967). While the results certainly suggested the existence of logical thinking ability as required in the Piaget-type tests, they also suggested that much of the performance in both the intelligence tests and the logical thinking experiments can be accounted for by a common intellectual ability. This would suggest that a child regarded as gifted on an IQ criterion would also be advanced in logical thinking.

It may be said, therefore, that the gifted child is likely to be at the same level of logical thinking as the average child three, four, or five years older.

References

BEARD, R. M. (1962). 'Children's reasoning', *Mathematics Teaching*, 21, pp. 33-9.

BERLYNE, D. E. (1957). 'Recent developments in Piaget's work', *Brit. J. Educ. Psychol.*, 27, pp. 1-12.

CASE, D. and COLLINSON, J. M. (1962). 'The development of formal thinking in verbal comprehension', *Brit. J. Educ. Psychol.*, 32, pp. 103-11.

ELKIND, D. (1961). 'Children's discovery of the conservation of mass, weight, and volume; Piaget replication study—II', *J. Genetic. Psychol.*, 98, pp. 219-27.

FLAVELL, J. H. (1963). *The Developmental Psychology of Jean Piaget*. London: Van Nostrand.

GETZELS, J. W. and JACKSON, P. W. (1962). *Creativity and Intelligence*, New York. Wiley.

GOLDMAN, R. J. (1962). *Some Aspects of the Development of Religious Thinking in Childhood and Adolescence.* Ph.D. thesis, University of Reading.

GUILFORD, J. P. (1959). 'Three faces of intellect', *Amer. Psychol.*, Vol. 14, pp. 469-78.

HALLAM, R. (1967). 'Logical thinking in history', *Educ. Review*, Vol. 19, No. 3, pp. 183-202.

HUGHES, M. M. (1965). 'A four-year longitudinal study of the growth of logical thinking in a group of secondary modern schoolboys'. Unpublished M.Ed. thesis, University of Leeds.

INHELDER, B. and PIAGET, J. (1958). *The Growth of Logical Thinking from Childhood of Adolescence.* London: Routledge & Kegan Paul.

INHELDER, B. (1964). 'Some aspects of Piaget's genetic approach to cognition'. In: COHEN, J., ed. *Readings in Psychology.* London: Allen & Unwin; pp. 93-4.

LODWICK, A. R. (1948). 'An investigation of the question whether the inferences that children draw in learning history correspond to the stages of mental development that Piaget postulates'. Diploma in Education dissertation, University of Birmingham. Unpublished.

LOVELL, K. (1961a). 'A follow-up study of Inhelder and Piaget's "The Growth of Logical Thinking" ', *Brit. J. Educ. Psychol.*, 52, pp. 143-55.

LOVELL, K. (1961b). *The Growth of Basic Mathematical and Scientific Concepts in Children.* London: University of London Press.

LOVELL, K. and OGILVIE, E. (1961). 'The growth of the concept of volume in junior school children', *J. Child Psychol. Psychiat.*, Vol. 2, pp. 118-26.

LOVELL, K. and BUTTERWORTH, I. B. (1966). 'Abilities underlying the understanding of proportionality', *Mathematics Teaching*, 37, pp. 5-9.

LOVELL, K. and SHIELDS, J. B. (1967). 'Some aspects of a study of the gifted child', *Brit. J. Educ. Psychol.*, 37, pp. 201-9.

LUNZER, E. A. (1960). 'Some points of Piagetian theory in the light of experimental criticism', *J. Child Psychol. Psychiat.*, Vol. 1, No. 3, pp. 191-202.

LUNZER, E. A. and PUMPHREY, P. D. (1966). 'Understanding proportionately', *Mathematics Teaching*, 34, pp. 7-13.

PIAGET, J. (1950). *The Psychology of Intelligence.* London: Routledge & Kegan Paul.

WALLACE, J. G. (1965). *Concept Growth and the Education of the Child.* Slough: NFER.

Chapter Five

Educating the Gifted Child

DISCUSSION on the education of gifted children is frequently concerned with the desirability of making proper provision for the children's needs. The matter has been raised by Parkyn (1948), James (1961), Waddington (1961), and by Burt (1962).

From time to time, special measures have been taken in various countries. In the case of children of outstanding intellectual ability, they have included the establishment of some form of 'ability grouping', either in special schools or in special classes in the regular school; the adoption of a system of 'acceleration' in which a child is placed in the same class as pupils a number of years older, and the development of a programme of 'enrichment' in which various means are used to provide pupils with opportunities for more advanced study than can be undertaken by the other members of the class.

Of the research workers whose studies have been described, Terman was concerned to find facts rather than to make suggestions for educational practice. In *The Promise of Youth* (1930), he wrote: 'It is the characteristics—physical, intellectual, social and moral—which we have attempted to delineate'. Parkyn, on the other hand, was very concerned about educational provision for highly intelligent children. He did not favour the idea of placing children in special schools, and thought that while 'acceleration' was permissible, it should only be done after very careful consideration of the whole personality of the child. He wrote strongly in support of an 'enriched curriculum'. He also thought that various forms of 'ability grouping' would be necessary, and advocated methods of teaching which would encourage children to think and solve problems for themselves rather than merely to acquire facts. Burt (1962) has writtenthat he recognizes the great duty we have of educating the 'vast mass of the population', and of 'providing extra help and extra care for the subnormal and the handicapped', but he has also asserted the vital importance of doing all we can todevelophigh ability. He has more recently (1967) suggested that there should be a special school for the mathematically gifted.

With artistically-gifted children, special provision is frequently delayed until the secondary stage of education but younger children may be encouraged and guided both by the regular class teacher and by a peripatetic specialist teacher. There are also schools where entry is restricted to children with very exceptional ability, such as The Royal Ballet School at Windsor and the Yehudi Menuhin School at Stoke d'Abernon. Many of the arrangements for gifted children are described and discussed in *Concepts of Excellence in Education* (Year Book of Education, 1961), *The Gifted Child* (Year Book of Education, 1962), by Wall (1960a, 1960b), by W. K. Durr in *The Gifted Student* (1964) and by M. J. Gold (1965) in *Education of the Intellectually Gifted.*

Some indication of the present view in Britain of the education of gifted children is given in the recent Plowden report, *Children and their Primary Schools*, published by the Department of Education and Science, which states: 'The needs of the highly gifted, however we define them, must be met'. Most members of the Plowden Committee thought that special schools should be restricted to those providing training in such arts as music and ballet, and that, except in the case of exceptional children who should be transferred to the next stage of education, the gifted child would be satisfactorily catered for in a good primary school. The Committee recognized the need for a richer curriculum and suggested various ways of supplying it, including the provision of a good library, and of television and radio programmes. The Report also suggested that assistance might be obtained from local people such as architects, physicists and artists, and showed how arrangements have been made for children to receive more specialized teaching at other educational institutions and at special centres on a voluntary and part-time basis.

There remains, however, the question of the contribution of the teacher in the school. He or more often she, makes a substantial and direct contribution to the education of the child, and also exercises some control over other agencies which may be employed. It is, therefore, imperative that the teacher should be sensitive to the abilities and interests of gifted children, and should be competent to decide on the best method of helping them to develop those abilities. While it is not the intention in this book to open up the whole question of teaching procedures, it is perhaps appropriate to suggest some of the implications of the study reported by Lovell and Shields.

The scores on the tests of intellectual abilities show that the thinking of the intellectually gifted child is characterized by high ability in observation, memory, reasoning, relational thinking and the knowledge and use of words, and that this ability is available in many situations. The needs of the child are likely to be best provided for if he is able to use this ability on as many occasions as possible. The good teacher will seek to provide him with many suitable experiences and activities over a wide curriculum, and make available to him many imaginative and informative books on a wide variety of topics.

The results of the investigation into the relationship between convergent and divergent thinking do not support the proposition that divergent thinking tasks measure an intellectual ability which exists entirely independent of IQ. There is, however, sufficient evidence of some divergent thinking abilities to suggest that teachers might provide for the development of divergent thinking when planning programmes for their classes, although it must be said that we do not know with any degree of precision the relevance of performance in divergent thinking tasks to performance in school and life tasks. But parts of the school curriculum, especially the parts with a considerable verbal element, could be presented so as to facilitate the development of fluency, flexibility and originality of thought. Fluency might be fostered if the teacher encouraged the continuance rather than the closure of thought; flexibility might develop if the individual teacher's programme and, indeed, the whole curriculum could demonstrate the inter-relatedness of subjects; originality might increase if pupils were given opportunities to find and organize data for themselves; indeed, experience in this form of learning might initiate spontaneous behaviour of the kind apparently adopted by the children studied by Piaget in Geneva, but not found generally among the children studied here. It is likely that the adoption of these suggestions would affect, not only the general structure of 'lessons', but the teacher's style and also the books which the pupils read and the learning tasks which they are set and also the design of school building.

The finding that only occasionally were the gifted children capable of formal thought in Piaget's sense of the term, suggests that even for these highly able children, learning experiences should have their roots in concrete situations. On the other hand, a most important issue is raised by the finding that many of the children were well advanced in concrete operations, and that a few of them were at times capable of formal thought. It is commonly held that the gifted child will teach himself, and that all that the teacher has to do is to provide the books. It may be that this is a quite inadequate procedure for facilitating the development of formal thought. It is suggested, therefore, that the gifted child of junior school age should be provided not only with imaginative and informative books on a wide variety of topics, and with rich concrete experiences over a wide curriculum, but that also he should have teachers who understand and keep in mind his stage of development and who can question his interpretations of data in many fields and thereby lead him to re-examine his arguments.

It is clear from the ratings made by the teachers that in their opinion the possession of high intelligence is not as a rule associated with poor general personality development, nor with any form of social disapproval in school. In fact the contrary is the case.

All teachers need to recognize the individual needs of their pupils, and teachers who are dealing with 'mixed ability' classes are particularly challenged by the demands of a wide variety of children. It has been my firm hope, in writing this book, to help them to understand the characteristics and thinking of the gifted child and to foster a concern for his welfare and development.

References

BEREDAY, G. Z. F. and LAUWERYS, J. A., eds. (1961). *Concepts of Excellence in Education. The Year Book of Education, 1961.* London: Evans.

BEREDAY, G. Z. F. and LAUWERYS, J. A., eds. (1962). *The Gifted Child. The Year Book of Education, 1962.* London: Evans.

BURT, C. (1962). 'General introduction: the gifted child'. In: BEREDAY, G. Z. F. and LAUWERYS, J. A., eds. *The Year Book of Education, 1962.* London: Evans.

BURT, C. (1967). 'Critical notice', *Brit. J. Educ. Psychol.*, 37, pp. 143-9.

DEPARTMENT OF EDUCATION AND SCIENCE: CENTRAL ADVISORY COUNCIL FOR EDUCATION (ENGLAND). (1967). *Children and their Primary Schools.* (Plowden Report). London: H.M. Stationery Office.

DURR, W. K. (1964). *The Gifted Student.* New York: Oxford University Press.

GOLD, M. J. (1965). *Education of the Intellectually Gifted.* Columbus, Ohio: Charles E. Merrill Books Inc.

LORD JAMES OF RUSHOLME. (1961). 'School and society in the education of the gifted: a British viewpoint'. In: BEREDAY, G. Z. F. and LAUWERYS, J. A., eds. *The Year Book of Education, 1961.* London: Evans.

LOVELL, K. and SHIELDS, J. B. (1967). 'Some aspects of a study of the gifted child', *Brit. J. Educ. Psychol.*, 37, pp. 201-8.

PARKYN, G. W. (1948). *Children of High Intelligence. A New Zealand Study.* New Zealand Council for Educational Research. London: Oxford University Press.

TERMAN, L. M., *et al.* (1930). *The Promise of Youth.* Stanford, Calif: Stanford University Press.

WADDINGTON, M. (1961). 'Problems of educating gifted young children with special reference to Britain', (Section II, Ch. I). In: BEREDAY, G. Z. F. and LAUWERYS, J. A., eds. *The Year Book of Education, 1961.* London: Evans.

WALL, W. D. (1960a). 'Highly intelligent children. Part I—The psychology of the gifted', *Educ. Res.*, Vol. II, No. 2, pp. 101-10.

WALL, W. D. (1960b). 'Highly intelligent children. Part II—The education of the gifted', *Educ. Res.*, Vol. II, No. 3, pp. 207-17.

Index